# Crossings

War Memories of Major Jerome T. Berry and the 19th Engineer
Regiment (Combat) in North Africa, Sicily and Italy, 1940 - 1945

By
**Major Jerome T. Berry &
Lieutenant Colonel Robert T. Berry**

# Crossings

**This book is dedicated to the 59 men of the 19th Engineer Regiment (Combat) who lost their lives during World War II. They are, as follows:**

| Tunisia | Sicily | Italy |
|---|---|---|
| **A Company:** | **D Company** | **A Company** |
| Pfc Stanley Borez | 1Lt Charles Ellis, Jr. | Pfc Eugene Davidson |
| Pvt Robert K. Kuehn | | 1Lt Edward Dufault |
| Pvt Earl W. Leakey | **F Company** | Pvt Willie Edens |
| | 2Lt John F. Hanrahan | S/Sgt Joseph Macuk |
| **B Company** | 2Lt Wilson V. Withers | Pvt Harry T. Penn |
| S/Sgt Lewis C. Mathews | | 1Lt William M. Rascoe |
| | | Tec5 William Wilson |
| **C Company** | | Pfc William Zimmerman |
| Pfc Kenneth L. Blanton | | |
| 1Lt Ward Dunham | | **B Company** |
| Cpl Ray C. Hughes | | Tec5 Ernest Decobellis |
| Pvt James Newman | | Pvt Mills M. Mraz |
| Pvt Erhardt H. Pischel | | Sgt Garret Visscher |
| Cpl Steve L. Tonsick | | |
| Pvt Bernard F. Uszcienski | | **C Company** |
| | | Pfc Edward Cichaczewski |
| **D Company** | | Pvt Joseph Covault |
| Pfc Merle R. Jorgenson | | 2Lt Wilho A. Seeronen |
| | | Pfc Lewis Foris |
| **E Company** | | Pvt Cecil Sledge |
| Tec5 George C. Rasek | | |
| Sgt Walter W. Smith | | **D Company** |
| | | Pvt Salvatore Bommarito |
| **F Company** | | Pfc Lennis Moore |
| Pvt Clarence Fulton | | Cpl Ray Oakley |
| Tec5 Barney Sandretto | | |
| Tec5 Charles D. Young | | **E Company** |
| | | Tec5 Milton Birnbaum |
| **H/S Company** | | Pvt Joseph Caltagirone |
| Pfc Grover Dunn | | Pfc Norman Duncan |
| | | Tec5 Murray Moore |
| | | Tec4 Chester Morris |
| | | Cpl Edgar Williams |
| | | |
| | | **F Company** |
| | | 1Lt James G. Brinton |
| | | Pfc Charles O. Erwin |
| | | Tec5 Wendell Maxham |
| | | Pvt Bernard O'Connor |
| | | 1Sgt Ray Palmquist |
| | | Pvt Clinton Powell |
| | | Pfc Peter T. Rekdal |
| | | Pfc Alfonso Rocco |
| | | Pfc William Rocco |
| | | Pvt Floyd E. Wilder |
| | | |
| | | **H/S Company** |
| | | Pfc Fred R. Gerdes |
| | | Cpt Otto Heye |
| | | Pfc Philibert Tetrault |

First Published in the Unites States of America, 2005
First American Edition, 2005
All rights reserved.

Copyright pending.

# Also by Robert T. Berry

**<u>Mud, Blood and Strawberries</u>,** The Illustrated Diary of Corporal Walter L. Strawhun, 1st Division, American Expeditionary Force, 1917 – 1919, available at Amazon.com

**<u>The Album of My Life</u>,** The Illustrated Life of Mary Frances Strawhun Berry

*"He's a recent high school graduate; he was probably an average student, pursued some form of sport activities, drives a ten-year old jalopy, and has a steady girlfriend that either broke up with him when he left, or swears to be waiting when he returns from half a world away. He listens to Benny Goodman, or hip-hop, or rock and roll or heavy metal or Mozart and the song of a 155mm howitzer. He is 10 or 15 pounds lighter now than when he was at home because he is working or fighting from before dawn to well after dusk.*

*He has trouble spelling thus letter writing is a pain for him, but he can field strip a rifle in 30 seconds and reassemble it in less time in the dark. He can recite to you the nomenclature of a machine gun or grenade launcher and use either one effectively if he must. He digs foxholes and latrines and can apply first aid like a professional. He can march until he is told to stop or stop until he is told to march.*

*He obeys orders instantly and without hesitation, but he is not without spirit or individual dignity. He is self-sufficient. He has two sets of fatigues: he washes one and wears the other. He keeps his canteens full and his feet dry. He sometimes forgets to brush his teeth, but never to clean his rifle. He can cook his own meals, mend his own clothes, and fix his own hurts. If you're thirsty, he'll share his water with you; if you are hungry, his food. He'll even split his ammunition with you in the midst of battle if you run low.*

*He seems to be always crossing something - oceans, rivers, minefields, beaches, deserts, mountains, frozen fields, muddy roads, swamps, jungles, bombed-out cities, and no-man's land, while someone is shooting at him - because as soon as he defeats the enemy of freedom, he can go home.*

*He has learned to use his hands like weapons and weapons like they were his hands. He can save your life - or take it, because that is his job. He will often do twice the work of a civilian, draw half the pay and still find ironic humor in it all. He has seen more suffering and death then he should have in his short lifetime.*

*He has stood atop mountains of dead bodies, and helped to create them. He has wept in public and in private, for friends who have fallen in combat and is unashamed. He feels every note of the National Anthem vibrate through his body while at rigid attention and while tempering the burning desire to 'square-away' those around him who haven't bothered to stand, remove their hat, or even stop talking. In an odd twist, day in and day out, far from home, he defends their right to be disrespectful.*

*Just as did his father, grandfather, and great-grandfather, he is paying the price for our freedom. Beardless or not, he is not a boy. He is the American Fighting Man that has kept this country and many others, free for over 200 years.*

*He has asked nothing in return, except our friendship, understanding, a short lull, a little shade and a picture of loved ones in his helmet. Remember him, always, for he has earned our respect and admiration with his blood."*

Anonymous

# To my Dad

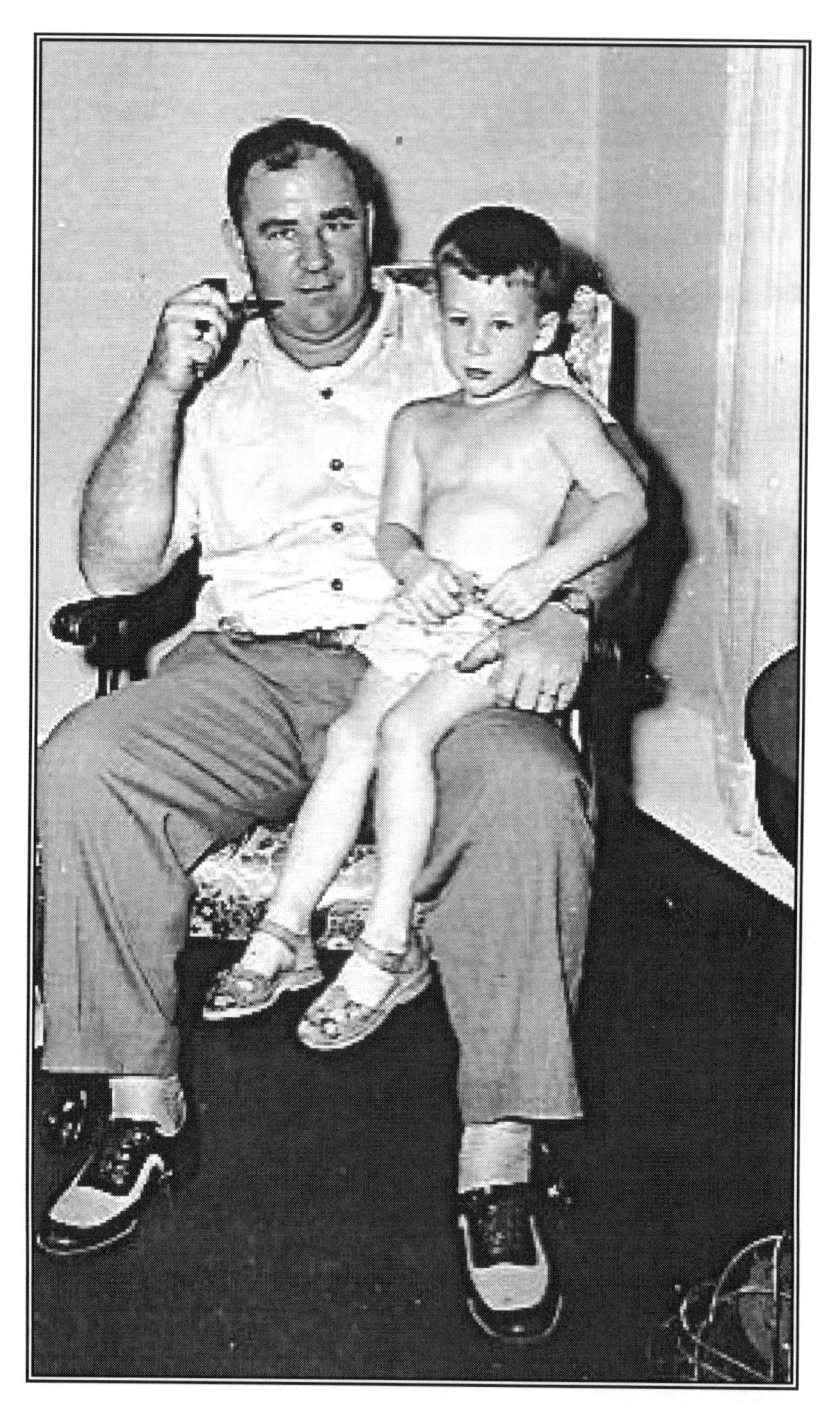

May 29, 1919 – July 8, 2005

# Crossings

War Memories of Major Jerome T. Berry and the 19th Engineer Regiment (Combat) in North Africa, Sicily and Italy, 1940 - 1945

# Contents

| | |
|---|---|
| Prologue | 1 |
| Early Years | 6 |
| World War II Begins | 11 |
| Basic Training and OCS | 16 |
| Great Britain | 29 |
| North Africa | 36 |
| Operation Torch | 39 |
| The Battle of Kasserine Pass | 66 |
| Invasion of Sicily | 102 |
| Invasion of Italy | 120 |
| The Battle of Monte Cassino | 140 |
| On to the Po River | 165 |
| Coming Home | 180 |
| Epilogue | 185 |
| References | 196 |

The mission of the combat engineers in time of war is to enable their armies to cross barriers when on the offensive, and to stop enemy armies from crossing barriers when the enemy is on the offensive. To accomplish this mission, combat engineers install mine fields, and blow up bridges, when the Army calls for them to slow the enemy's advance. When on the offensive, combat engineers cross mine fields, re-build bridges, build rafts and floating bridges and enable the army to cross natural barriers or those erected by the enemy.

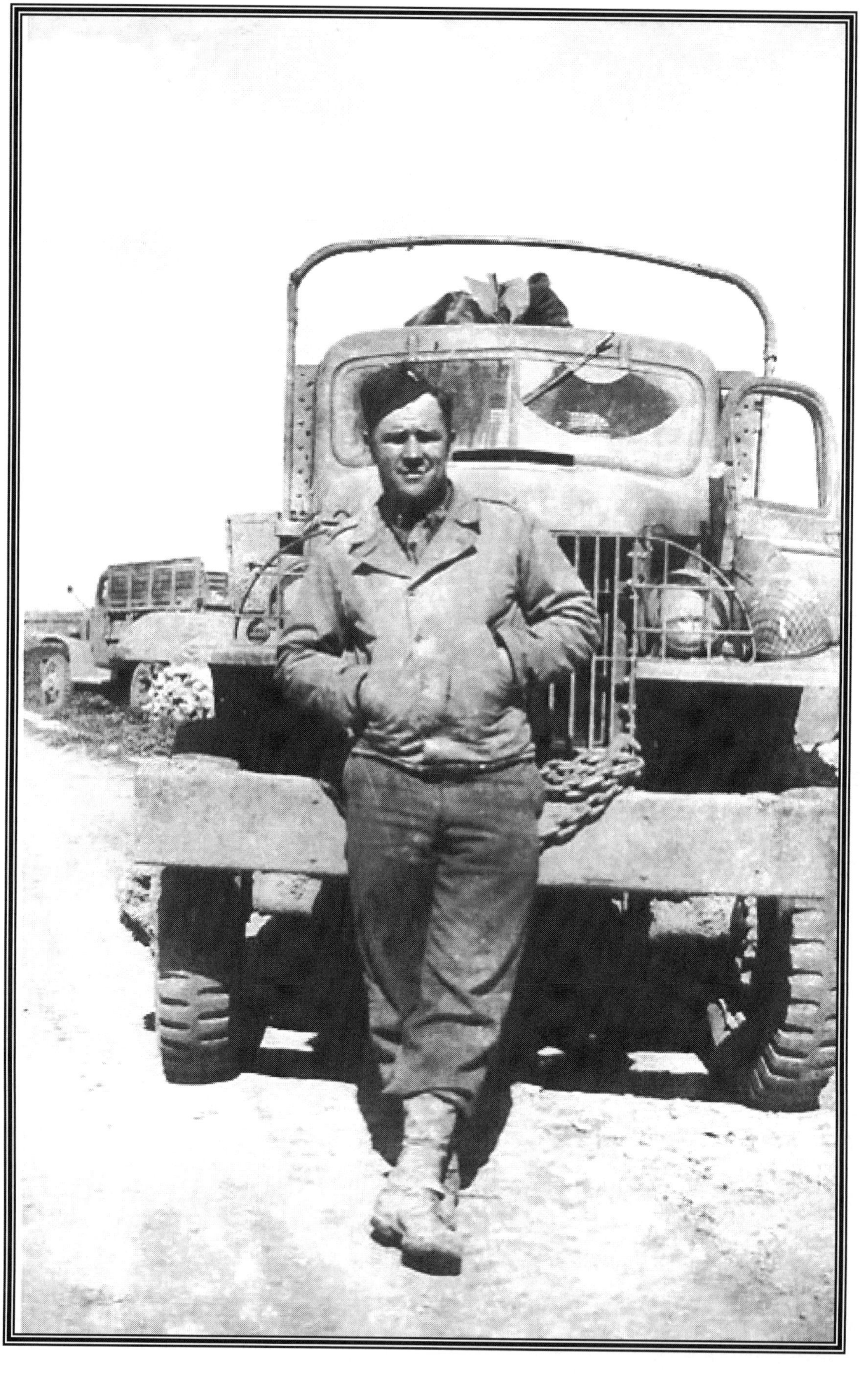

# Prologue

Like most veterans of World War II, dad didn't talk too much about the war. There was mention of an occasional war buddy and monthly reminders of his army life when he attended weekend reserve meetings. Once in a while when I was a kid, he convinced me to polish his army boots for him before a drill weekend. On several occasions, our family went with dad and his unit for "summer camp" as our summer vacation. During the summer of 1964, we all went to Fort Carson where dad did his reserve duties while my sister and I went to the pool or played golf or went to a movie. But even in that setting, there were no war stories.

One of my most vivid memories as a kid was going to the officer's club at nearby Fort Leonard Wood on special occasions. I not only got a kick out of seeing army trainees in action, but the best part was eating the biggest hamburgers I'd ever seen. But still, there were no war stories.

On at least three occasions our family traveled to a 19th Engineer Regiment (Combat) reunion. Long car trips to Michigan or Wisconsin seemed like they would take forever. Of course, other than dad, my mom, my sister and I didn't know another soul there so we had to be on our best behavior and try to have fun in the midst of all of these boring meetings and parties. I'm sure there were lots of war stories at those reunions, but I was never around to hear them or, if I was, I didn't pay attention to them.

COMPANY "F"
**Seated L-R:** Larry Wehrle, Dick Widelski, Bill Gugel. **Standing L-R:** Bob Williams, Ed Pohlmann & Jerry Berry.
*Photo taken of members of Company F who attended the 1989 19th Engineer Regiment reunion.*

In the early 1980's Bob Weed's book about the 19th Engineer Regiment, "In Time of War" came out and I remember dad talking about it, but I didn't read it and, although it provoked silent memories in dad, he didn't relive them to us.

Meanwhile, boxes of photographs, old letters, tattered books and memorabilia got packed away in musty basements. Photographs curled and molded; letters disappeared; memories got lost. In high school, for some unknown reason, I found the Nazi helmet that Dad had brought back from Italy and spray painted it gold, essentially ruining it. The helmet originally belonged to Sergeant Kurtz, who had written his name in the liner, and who presumably didn't live to tell war stories either.

In 1994, I wrote a book about my grandfather's time as a truck driver in the 1$^{st}$ Infantry Division in World War I. As I completed that effort, I started thinking about doing the same thing for my dad. But, time passed and the busy days of raising children and attending swim meets and advancing a career seemed to always get in the way. In 1997, my mother died and I started becoming closer than ever to my dad. Finally, in the fall of 2003, I started recording the first of six video tapes of my dad telling the story of his time in the army, and, finally, some war stories.

HEADQUARTERS COMPANY
Jerry Berry, George Winzeler & Reuben Gilles.

I started assembling the book in the fall of 2004. Dad and I went through over 200 photographs and he worked to remember names and places and dates. It was amazing how good his memory was of those years – surely a testament to how important those days were in his life. There were a few tears as he remembered his driver, Clarence Fulton, getting killed during the Battle of Kasserine Pass and his best buddies, Lieutenants Charlie Ellis, Wilson Withers and John Hanrahan getting killed by a mine in Sicily. It is such a joy to write a book. You are able to stir your creative juices and you learn so much about your subject. Writing a book with your Dad about your Dad is about the best thing there is. You learn about your Dad. You close the loop. You feel fulfilled. You finish what he started. You realize his greatness. You understand his shortcomings. You appreciate his sacrifice. You stir your soul. You imagine him as a young man on a dangerous, honorable adventure. You feel him dirty and sweaty and smelly from days in combat. You taste his hunger from weeks of nothing but C rations; you feel his thirst in the North African desert. You feel the sand in his food, the mud on his clothes and you hear the laughter from the many nights of comradeship with his buddies. You think of him recovering in a hospital after being wounded. You sense his emotion as he watched hundreds of tons of bombs being dropped on Monte Cassino. You touch his heart. But, more important, he touches yours.

You see photographs of him standing in the mud, eating in a tent, drinking wine on R&R, standing by a dead Nazi, talking to Tunisians, leading his platoon, carrying a dead American pilot, relaxing on the beach, building a bridge, sitting on a jeep and getting a Bronze Star pinned on his chest. You hear him tell the same war stories over and over; you feel his pain; you feel his pride; you learn about him as a man. You read letters sent home to his "girl"; you feel his excitement and you understand his fear. You relive his nightmares and realize his dreams.

You get to finally, finally, tell his story.

Armies must cross obstacles as they advance as well as place obstacles as they retreat. That has been the mission of combat engineers since the beginning of modern warfare. Combat engineers enable Armies to cross minefields, rivers, mountains and deserts, all while fighting as infantry when the need arises.

This book is about the men of the 19th Engineer Regiment (Combat), a unit of the II Corps of the US

Army during World War II. The 19th crossed the United States, the Atlantic Ocean, the Mediterranean Sea, Algeria, Tunisia, Sicily and Italy. They fought and died as they crossed Kasserine Pass, the Rapido River and the Liri Valley. All along the way, they crossed mine fields, built bridges, repaired railroad lines, built gun emplacements, repaired roads and constructed rafts. They fought as infantry at Kasserine Pass, and at El Guettar and at Monte Cassino. They fought, worked and died to enable the United States Army to continue its advance on the Axis powers of Germany and Italy. Fifty-nine soldiers of the 19th died along the way. Some, like Clarence Fulton, Alphonso Rocco, Charlie Ellis, John Hanrahan and Wilson Withers, were close friends of Jerry Berry. This is their story.

When dad and I put together this book in 2004, we looked at hundreds of photographs and reviewed a number of reference books. Some of the photographs were captioned, many were not. Dad tried to remember names of everyone, but after sixty years, memories of names fade. Our deepest apologies to anyone who we misnamed or gave the wrong rank or could not identify in a photo, or to anyone to whom we attributed some experience that is false, exaggerated or, plain wrong. We both did our best.

We both hope that you enjoy this war story.

*Lt. Berry, near Bizerte, July 1943. His II Corps shows proudly on his left sleeve.*

*Jerry and his Mom doing the wash on the farm in Tupelo, Arkansas, 1920.*

# Early Years

Jerry Berry's father, Clarence Washington Berry was born in Redfield, Arkansas near Hot Springs on March 7, 1894. Later, the Berry family moved to Benton, Arkansas. Clarence's father, Walter Scott Berry, farmed and worked in a saw mill near Benton. He did much of the fine finish for wood cabinets and other wood products.

*The girls from the deaf school in Little Rock. Fannie Taylor is third from the right and her future sister-in-law, Ella Berry, second from right.*

In early 1900, there was a scarlet fever epidemic in the county and many children, including Clarence, were infected with the disease. Because of this illness, he lost his hearing and became deaf-mute. Soon thereafter, he was enrolled in a school for the deaf in Little Rock, Arkansas where he continued his schooling until he graduated. While there, he learned the trade of a tailor.

While he was in school in Little Rock, he met Fannie Cornelia Taylor, who also had been stricken with scarlet fever. Fannie was from Tupelo, Arkansas where her father farmed.

On September 2, 1917, after they graduated from high school, Clarence Berry and Fannie Taylor were married in Tupelo, Arkansas. Clarence opened a shop there providing cleaning and pressing and tailoring. Fannie tended the garden and raised chickens and they began to plan a family.

*Clarence Berry's tailor shop in Tupelo, Arkansas, around 1918.*

The first addition to their family was Jerome Taylor Berry who was born on May 29, 1919 in Tupelo in the family residence. As both of his parents were deaf-mute, neighbors had to teach him how to talk while he learned to communicate with his parents through signing.

On November 11, 1918, World War I was over and America's industrial potential ignited. Industry flourished and one of the biggest and newest industries was the automobile industry.

Earlier, BF Goodrich had founded a small rubber factory in Akron and now that Detroit auto makers needed more and more tires, Goodrich's plant in Akron took off. Soon, other tire-makers, including Goodyear, Firestone and General, also opened major manufacturing plants in Akron. Akron became the rubber tire capital of the world.

Working in a rubber tire plant was conducive to many people who were deaf because of the noise that the process produced. Deaf people flocked to Akron to work in the tire plants, including many classmates from the deaf school in Little Rock as well as friends of both Clarence and Fannie Berry

In 1920, after a number of letters, the Berry's decided to move their tailor business to Akron to take advantage of the boom in the city and to be with other deaf people there. So, off they went, from Tupelo, Arkansas to Akron, Ohio, Clarence, Fannie and one-year old Jerome.

*Fannie Berry and her new baby boy, Jerome, taken in Tupelo, Arkansas, summer 1919.*

Upon arrival in Akron, Clarence got a job with the Read-Benzol Company which was an industrial fabric cleaning company. The company cleaned drapes and other expensive fabrics for the wealthy property owners and hotels of Akron. Clarence started as a "presser" and soon became the manager of the pressing operation. He also worked as a tailor on the side. Soon after arrival, the Berry's rented a home in what is called Goodyear Heights, a subdivision built by the Goodyear Company for its workers.

Jerome and the other Berry kids grew up in Akron in the Goodyear Heights neighborhood and attended public schools there. But, just as Clarence was born in 1929, the great stock market crash occurred and the Great Depression began. In 1930 (or so), things were so difficult for the Berry family that a decision was made to send Jerome back to Arkansas to live with extended family there in order to be able to afford to take care of the rest of the family. So, just after he turned 11 in the early summer of 1930, Jerome left Akron and headed back to Tupelo.

*Jerry in a" dress" and his mother in Akron, around 1922.*

There, he first lived with his grandmother Taylor and then moved in with his uncle, Charlie Taylor on his farm outside of Tupelo. He remained living with his uncle during the school year in 1931 and after school was over, he moved in with his uncle Boyce Taylor for the rest of the summer.

At the end of summer, 1931, Jerome moved back to Akron to be with his family and to start the seventh grade. He completed junior high school and graduated from East Akron High in 1937, where he played football. That summer, his high school coach arranged for him to get a scholarship to play football at Akron University. Jerome enrolled there as a freshman in the fall of 1937. He played varsity football and attended college at Akron U. during the 1937-38 school year and the fall semester of 1938. He also enrolled in R.O.T.C. and took military classes and close order drill while there. However, his money ran out and he was not able to continue college for the spring semester of 1939. At that time, Jerry worked at a men's store in Akron called O'Neil's Department Store and flipped hamburgers at Kewpie's, an Akron burger establishment.

In fact, Jerry worked at Kewpie's most of the time while he was in college at Akron. Many times, he had to work the night shift, starting work at 8:00 PM. His boss would let him off a few minutes early in order to make class that began at 8:00 AM. He would have to go to class after being up all night and smelling of fried onions and hamburger meat.

*Jerry and his scooter, Akron, Ohio, 1923.*

There were few jobs and less money as the depression was at its lowest point. During this time, Jerry lived at home and tried to make ends meet while still dreaming of playing college football and finishing college. World War II started on September 1, 1939 when Germany attacked Poland and Poland's allies, Great Britain and France, declared war on Germany. In the spring of 1940, as the war in Europe waged, the Akron U. coach, accepted a job as the head football coach at the University of Nevada at Reno (UNR). He invited some of his Akron players, including Jerry, who

*The Berry Family, front row left to right, Clarence, Jerome, Katherine, Fannie; back row, Clarence's sister, Ella Berry, his brother, and his mother, taken in the summer of 1923.*

8

*Jerry Berry (in center) all dressed up with his pretty cool friends, around 1934 in Akron.*

hadn't played in the fall of '39, to come out west and join the UNR team.

As he recalls, he hitchhiked from Akron to Reno arriving August 1940. The coach had said, "if you can make it to Reno, I'll take care of you from there." Dad showed up at the coach's door with a lot of hunger, a small suitcase and an empty wallet, but the coach fulfilled the promise and provided a football scholarship.

Jerry pledged the Sigma Alpha Epsilon house in Reno and was initiated into that fraternity and lived there during the school year of 1940-41. He played varsity football, in the same backfield as Marion Motley who later played professional football and is in the NFL Hall of Fame. Jerry, however, got hurt and did not get too much playing time. He also continued his classes as a member of R.O.T.C. The spring of 1941, Jerry was on the varsity track team while he continued college.

Then, as his first year at UNR was ending in May of 1941, he was drafted into the Army. Jerry, along with other young men of the United States had reported to the Selective Service Administration and had registered for the draft. Although, he had also talked to the U.S. Navy about joining the Navy, the Army draft beat the Navy to Jerry's leadership and he was drafted into the Army.

On May 7, 1941, just as the semester at UNR was ending, Jerry was ordered to appear to the train station

*The Berry family, sans Jerry, about 1932. Katherine, Clarence and Laura in front; Clarence Sr. and Fannie in back.*

at Reno. Dozens of other young men were there when Jerry reported. Soon, a train came to the station and an Army sergeant told the group to get on the train. They traveled by train to Ogden, Utah and then by bus to Fort Douglas, Utah, located in the suburbs of Salt Lake City.

He arrived at Fort Douglas and was given an entrance physical there, which generally consisted of a determination if the draftee could walk and see. If so, he passed the physical. From Fort Douglas, Jerry was ordered onto another train – destination unknown. He and hundreds of other unsuspecting young draftees were loaded onto trains and off they went. As yet, the war had not reached the United States and many people were hopeful that the United States could stay out of the war. It was not to be.

*Jerry Berry's East Akron High School graduation photo, May 1937.*

*A college photo of Jerry Berry, around 1940, probably taken at UNR because he is wearing his fraternity pin.*

*German schoolgirls garlanded like Aryan goddesses give a salute to the Third Reich at a political rally in Germany, mid-1930's. (14.)*

# World War II Begins

On September 1, 1939, Germany invaded Poland which, to most historians, marked the start of World War II. The devastation of World War II caused the deaths of over 27,600 people per day for the next 6 years. The Fascist government of Nazi Germany was allied with the Fascist governments of Italy and Japan to form the Axis Powers. Later, other Germanic countries such as Austria, Bulgaria, Romania, Hungary and Czechoslovakia, supplied fighting units for the Axis powers.

France and Great Britain had, meanwhile, previously signed a treaty with Poland. Because Germany invaded Poland, France and Great Britain ceremoniously declared war on Germany on September 3, 1940. However, the Allied powers were not yet prepared for war so there was little fighting after September 3rd until early April 1940 when the German army invaded and seized Denmark and Norway. A month later in early May, 1940, 136 German divisions swept into the Netherlands, Belgium, Luxembourg and France and drove the French, Dutch, Belgian and British armies into the sea at Dunkirk. On June 14th, German columns entered Paris and the European continent was completely under Nazi control.

Rather than continue fighting throughout the remainder of France, Germany signed a truce with the remnants of the French government which gave control of the southern 40% of France to the "Vichy French", so called because their seat of government was located in Vichy, France. The Vichy French were given control of their part of France as well as the French colonies of Morocco, Algeria and Tunisia if they allied with the Axis powers. Marshall Philippe Petain, the French hero of Verdun in WWI, was named as the 84-year-old leader of the Vichy French and he betrayed free France by pledging France's support to Hitler's Third Reich and the Axis alliance. Two years later, the Vichy French forces in North Africa, allied with the Axis Powers, would face American and British invasion of Morocco and Algeria and wreak havoc on allied forces, killing thousands before surrendering and changing sides.

*Adolf Hitler and Benito Mussolini in Berlin, 1937.*

Meanwhile, the US helped Great Britain by sending tanks, artillery, rifles, ships, airplanes and other supplies while Great Britain worked to get ready for war. In October 1940, Italy invaded Greece but their advance was weak and faltered so Germany reinforced Italy's forces to complete the conquest which was finally concluded in April 1941. Yugoslavia was next and although they put up a good fight, it also fell to the Axis powers in April 1941.

In Africa, Mussolini's legions attacked British forces in Egypt from Italy's colony in Libya. The Italians were severely trounced by the British but the Germans again came to their rescue and sent General Erwin

Rommel to salvage the Italians' advance. With his rear safely secured by his allies, the Vichy French, Rommel launched an attack in mid-February 1941 to the east from Libya and drove the British back to the outskirts of Cairo. The fighting in Libya and Egypt between the Germans and Italians against the British and Egyptians waged back and forth for nearly two years while the Allies planned their invasion of North Africa.

Then, two events happened in 1941 to eventually turn the tide against the Axis powers. First, on June 22, 1941, as Jerry Berry was in basic training at Fort Leonard Wood, Germany broke their alliance with the Soviet Union and launched a massive attack toward Moscow. Fighting was ferocious in western Russia in what became known in Germany as the Eastern Front, throughout the rest of the year and throughout 1942 through the end of the war. While Germany poured hundreds of divisions into the Eastern Front, their forces in Western Europe and North Africa were weakened.

Of course, on December 7, 1941, Japan attacked U.S. Naval forces at Pearl Harbor, Hawaii which was the second major event that turned the war against the Axis. Within a few days of the U.S. entering the war

*Italian anti-aircraft unit on alert during British counterattack in Egypt, February 1941 (14.)*

on the side of the British and her allies, Churchill arrived in Washington to begin strategic talks with

Roosevelt on the waging of the war against Germany. Timetables and logistics were cussed and discussed. U.S. strategists wanted to invade France and to fight directly toward Berlin to open an immediate western front in order to help relieve the pressure on Russia. However, the British had all too recent nightmares of WWI and the horrific trench warfare throughout eastern and northern France. Meanwhile the world waited for the Allies.

*German soldiers in Paris. (14.)*

The British, alternately, pressed for an invasion of North Africa prior to invading the continent of Europe in order to trap the German Afrika Korps between Montgomery's British Eighth Army in Egypt and the invasion forces in Algeria and Tunisia. Their theory was to start to encircle the Germans and to encourage uprisings in outlying areas of the Third Reich. In addition, Allied occupation of North Africa would re-open the Mediterranean to Allied shipping and provide a jumping-off place for an invasion of Italy through Sicily.

The Americans continued to disagree with this strategy asserting that a campaign in North Africa would be nothing more than a side show when the real enemy was deep in the heart of Europe. The Americans wanted to help the Russians by quickly opening a new front in Germany's rear in France. It was imperative to the Americans that the U.S. engage the enemy before the end of 1942 in order to support the Russians fighting on the Eastern front.

The war strategists of both Britain and the U.S. continued the argument from early 1942 through June of the same year. As the debate continued, the British were

*Roosevelt and Churchill confer, 1941. (14.)*

badly defeated by Rommel at Tobruk on June 21, 1942 at exactly the moment that Churchill was sitting in Roosevelt's Oval office. At that meeting, Roosevelt finally pledged support to the British plan but he still had to convince his military leaders who insisted on an invasion of Western Europe.

Finally, on July 25, 1942, Roosevelt announced to his staff that the U.S. would support the British in an invasion of North Africa, despite bitter opposition from his own military staff. Operation Torch, as the invasion of North Africa was now called, had been born. Roosevelt's decision remained controversial for decades as it still does today. However, the decision to invade North Africa provided the Allies time to better prepare for the invasion of Normandy and to give American commanders and units combat experience against the German Army.

***German soldiers on the Eastern front tending to one of their comrades who has just had his left arm shot off - it is laying in the foreground.***

15

# Basic Training and OCS

In May 1941, as Roosevelt and Churchill were debating the next step of the Allies, Berry and the other draftees at Fort Douglas reported to the train depot in Salt Lake City. There, several troop trains were being loaded with draftees and recruits. Upon arrival, the men were randomly divided and sent to different trains. There was no apparent plan or reason why men were loaded on certain trains. No one knew where any train was going or what was going to happen to them. Troop trains were sent to various training posts in the western U.S. Berry's train headed to Fort Leonard Wood, a brand-new post still under construction 120 miles southwest of St. Louis at the edge of the Ozark Mountains.

At first, the train headed south and southwest so many of the men thought that the train was headed for southern California, which delighted the men, many of whom were from the southern California area. However, during the night, while the men were trying to sleep, the train turned east and the morning

*Basic training in the mud at Fort Leonard Wood, Missouri, summer, 1941. Notice the "pup" tents and the mud surrounding them. Looks like a great time! It was during the early days of the fort that it became known as "Fort Lost-in-the-Woods".*

daylight revealed that the train was traveling east across Arizona. Some speculated that the train was headed for one of several posts in Texas, or, maybe, Fort Sill, Oklahoma or maybe, Fort Riley, Kansas. They continued traveling by train that day and that night. They passed the time playing cards or shooting craps or talking about their future plans for life in the Army.

*Buck Private Berry and friends during basic training at Ft. Leonard Wood, summer 1941. It looks like they may be eating some cake or cookies sent from home in a box.*

The next morning, around dawn, the train creaked to a stop at a sleepy little town. The men were ordered to get their gear and get off of the train. They asked where they were and were told that they were in Newburg, Missouri, a few miles from a new army post being constructed to Newburg's west. The men loaded into another train for a short but harrowing trip to the new post. On the way to the new post, the men discovered that they were on the first train to ever travel the spur to Fort Leonard Wood. In front of their train, they pushed a railroad car full of rock and tree trunks which was used to make sure that the new wooden trestles over the several creeks along the way were sufficiently designed and built.

The train arrived at Fort Wood mid-morning and the men were lined up and processed for duty. After receiving a small amount of uniforms and equipment, the men were moved into their barracks, which had only recently been constructed by civilian carpenters who were busy all over the post building the post for more trainees.

*Private Berry on the right, with a buddy, Ft. Leonard Wood, 1941.*

Instead of undergoing military training during basic training, the first arrivals at Fort Wood were set to building roads. They worked with hand-tools as well as equipment to construct roads from the main area of the fort to the banks of the Big Piney River, nearby.

*Pup tents in the mud for B company, 27th Basic Training Battalion, Ft. Wood, Fall 1941.*

Finally, in late summer 1941, the men began military training in marksmanship, close order drill and, of course, kitchen police (KP) duty. Jerry was immediately recognized by his superiors because he had two years of R.O.T.C. and could drill well and knew many of the basics in marching and command. He was made an acting platoon sergeant while still a private. He was assigned to B Company of the 27th Basic Training Battalion.

Every day, more and more barracks and other military buildings were built by some 20,000 carpenters reported to be on the post working. Buildings went up like weeds, while more and more trainees came in by train and bus to attend basic training. The men worked and trained day-in and day-out and finally finished basic training in late fall 1941 as the Japanese fleet was secretly sailing toward Pearl Harbor.

Weekend passes were spent discovering area bars and dance halls. One of the favorite towns nearby was Rolla, Missouri, where there was a USO and where USO dances were held.

When they weren't training, the men stood guard duty, had KP duty, cleaned the barracks and took care of their uniforms and equipment. Daily inspections made sure that the men were healthy and taking care of their gear.

After basic training ended, Jerry was promoted to private first class (one chevron, or stripe) along with the other graduates of B Company. It is standard that men in basic training are "buck" privates, meaning they have no rank, until they graduate from basic training. Upon graduation, the men are promoted to private (one stripe) and begin training in their assigned field, such as artillery, armor, infantry, etc. The men at Ft. Leonard Wood began their training in the engineer branch immediately after basic training.

For the engineer branch, training shifted to combat engineer training and classroom education on the engineer branch of the Army. They learned how to search for and clear mines, how to lay a mine field, how to build bridges, how to destroy bridges and how to operate engineer equipment such as bulldozers, scrapers, loaders, back hoes and dump trucks.

*Private Berry (kneeling, front center) and a few of his buddies posing in the company area at Ft. Wood, Missouri, August, 1941.*

*PFC Berry in front of the mess hall at Ft. Wood, Fall 1941.*

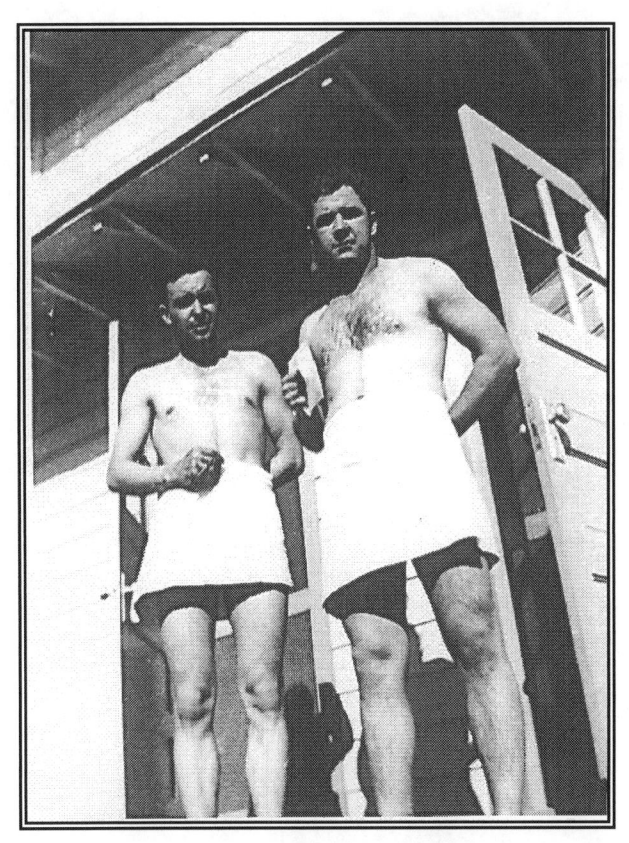

*Berry and his buddy at shower time during basic training, Ft. Wood, summer 1941.*

*Jerry Berry in the middle of the back seat with some of his friends during basic training at Fort Leonard Wood, Missouri. It was common to take a road trip to Rolla, Columbia or other nearby Missouri cities that may contain girls, whenever they could manage a pass. This was probably taken in the fall of 1941 during their Engineer Basic Course.*

After basic, the men could get passes on weekends. One weekend in October 1941 Jerry caught a ride to the University of Missouri campus in Columbia where he went to the SAE fraternity house and stayed for the weekend, reliving his college days that seemed so long ago.

Later, when he was back at Ft. Wood, they were told that a busload of girls from the University of Missouri were coming to the USO in Rolla for a dance. Jerry and three of his buddies drove to Rolla for the dance. When they got there, they discovered that there were already other soldiers there and that all of the girls were already dancing. About that time, Jerry noticed a pretty girl walking in the room with her mother at her side. Since the girl was the only one there (besides her mother) who wasn't dancing, Jerry went over, introduced himself and asked her to dance. He found out that her name was Mary Frances Strawhun and that she was from Rolla but went to school at the University of Missouri in Columbia and was a member of the Alpha Gamma Delta sorority. She told him that members of her sorority were there but since she had grown up in Rolla, in fact just across the street, that her mother wanted to come along, too.

Jerry and Mary Frances seemed to hit it off and both were good dancers, more so than most there. So, they ended up dancing together most of the night. That chance meeting, as is often the case, was the beginning of "something big", as they say. Jerry and Mary Fran exchanged letters all during the

*Pvt Berry in front of the movie theater at Fort Wood during the engineer basic course, Fall 1941.*

engineer course during the fall of 1941. Both managed to make it to Rolla for many weekends. During the week, scores of letters were written. Jerry remembers having Thanksgiving dinner with the Strawhun family, who were living on the corner of 7th and Rolla Streets in the fall of 1941.

Jerry stood out as potential officer material because of his natural military bearing, his leadership skills and his experience as an R.O.T.C. cadet at Akron and UNR. He discussed attending Officer Candidate School (OCS) at Fort Belvoir. The commander of training company B was Captain Davenport who was a career officer and who always carried a swagger stick. He encouraged Jerry to go to OCS when he finished branch training.

However, like many lives that day, Jerry and Mary Fran's lives were suddenly changed on Sunday, December 7, 1941. On that day, after a Saturday in Rolla seeing Mary Fran, Jerry and a few other men decided to take in a movie at one of the new post movie theaters.

The men were "issued" movie tickets at a cost of 11 tickets for a dollar, which was taken out of their pay whether they wanted the tickets or not. The men went to the theater and were watching a movie when the movie was stopped and a soldier went up on stage to read an announcement that the Japanese had bombed U.S. Naval forces at Pearl Harbor, Hawaii. Few of the men really understood the meaning of what they were hearing and few even knew of Pearl Harbor.

Soon, however, it was apparent that the United States was at war. There was an immediate call for more men in the armed forces and the United States Army needed additional officers to lead the thousands of new soldiers that were enlisting daily. Jerry was told that any man who had R.O.T.C. in college would be accepted into OCS. He immediately applied and was given a letter of recommendation by Captain Davenport. He was soon accepted, given orders and left for Fort Belvoir, Virginia by the end of 1941.

Corporal Berry saw Mary Frances in Rolla on his way to Fort Belvoir, Virginia in late December 1941. He advanced through OCS, graduating in March 1942 and was selected for the Engineer Branch. He then went to Engineer Officer Basic Course, also at Ft. Belvoir, and was in Class #2 of that course, graduating

*Private Berry (left) and a friend (right) hold a snake (middle) during basic training, 1941.*

*Second Lieutenant Berry shortly after graduating from Officer Candidate School, Spring 1942.*

*Pvt Berry ready for guard duty, Ft. Wood, 1941.*

*Mary Frances Strawhun as a sorority girl at the University of Missouri c. 1941.*

in May 1942. Prior to graduation, Jerry asked to be assigned to a combat engineer unit and upon graduation was assigned to the "601st COM Engineer Battalion" at Fort Ord, California, near Monterrey.

Upon arrival in late May 1942, 2Lt Berry discovered that there was a typographical error and he was actually assigned to the 601st CAM Engineer Battalion and the "CAM" stood for Camouflage. His unit designed and manufactured camouflage which was soon to be needed throughout the world to hide tanks and artillery pieces, as well as troop positions. The unit had a number of movie technicians from Hollywood who had the skills to create fake trucks and tanks from fabric and plywood. One of the major skills that had to be learned by the men was sewing as they had to use large sewing machines to make the camouflage netting.

While there, he helped make large wooden boxes out of plywood and netting that looked like tanks from a couple of hundred yards away or from the air. Thousands of these fake tanks were used in Great Britain and elsewhere to draw fire and aerial attacks from unwitting Axis forces.

Berry soon was disappointed with his assignment and requested transfer to a combat engineer unit. His wish was granted in early July 1942 when he was ordered to report to the 19th Engineer Regiment (Combat) which was located at that time at Pasadena, California in Oak Grove Park. He took a train from

*A tank made of plywood and cardboard by the men of the 601st Camouflage Battalion under the able direction of 1Lt Bob Cranmer and 2Lt Jerry Berry at Fort Ord, California, May 1942.*

Monterrey to Pasadena and took a cab to Oak Grove Park, which is the site of the Rose Bowl.

The Regiment was being formed and had use of the Rose Bowl to prepare defenses for the soon-expected Japanese invasion of southern California. The engineers were making concertina wire to protect machine gun emplacements on Monterrey Beach. The unit had large barb wire-making machines which were located inside of the Rose Bowl. The men would manufacture the barbed wire into rolls and then tie them in compressed bundles and take them to the gun positions along the beach. Six months after the destruction at Pearl Harbor, it was expected that the Japanese would invade California at any time so the military was manning the gun positions 24 hours a day to defend the shores of the United States. Of course, it was ridiculous to imagine that a few machine guns and barb wire could stop a real invasion but this was the hysteria that was prevalent in the United States at that time.

*19th Engineer Regiment on parade while at Pasadena, California, 1942.*

All of southern California was under black-out conditions so the men had to work at night in the dark to make the concertina strands.

It was at Pasadena when Jerry met several of the other officers of the 19th that he would work and fight with during the next three years. Upon arrival, 2Lt Berry was assigned as the platoon leader of 1st Platoon of F Company in the 2nd Battalion of the 19th Engineer Regiment. F Company was commanded by 1Lt Edgar Pohlman. Soon after arrival more officers reported to duty with the 19th including 2Lts Charles E. (Charlie) Ellis and Robert C. (Bob) Weed who were assigned as 2nd Platoon and 3rd Platoon leaders, respectively.(1.) (Ellis would be killed later in Sicily while Weed would remain Berry's friend for life. Pohlman served as Berry's best man four years later as the war was ending.)

*Second Lieutenant Berry, probably taken at Ft. Belvoir, spring 1942.*

Morale was high in the 19th. Although the war was going badly for the Allies in both Europe and in the Pacific, the men of the 19th knew that they would end up playing an important role in the eventual defeat of the Axis powers. All seemed eager to get to the fighting, which most believed they would see in the Pacific theater of operations against the Japanese.

Jerry spent a couple of weeks in Pasadena when, one morning in early July 1942 the 19th Engineer Regiment was ordered to report to Camp Kilmer, New Jersey. The regiment was loaded on a train in Los Angeles and started south. Many of the men, who hadn't been told of their destination, assumed that the unit was headed for troop ships that would take them to the Pacific theater. However, the train soon turned east and the men spent several days chugging east to New Jersey through Arizona, Kansas and, finally, to Chicago.

The train was full of soldiers, crammed into every corner like sardines in a can. There was no air conditioning and the train was sticky with sweat in the July heat and the men were hungry and bored. The officers spent most of their time on an open baggage car that doubled as the company kitchen, as it was the coolest place to be. After about three days of travel, the train made a stop at Ft Wayne, Indiana.

Bob Weed (1.) remembers that when the train stopped many of the men were allowed to get off to stretch

**CUNARD WHITE STAR LINER "QUEEN ELIZABETH"**
THE LARGEST SHIP IN THE WORLD.—Length: 1,030 feet, 12 feet longer than the "Queen Mary." Length of Prom. Deck: 724 feet. Breadth: 118 feet. Depth to top of Lounge structure: 120 feet. Number of Decks: 14. Gross tonnage (Approx.) 85,000. Built by John Brown & Co. Ltd., Clydebank. Date of Launch: Tuesday, September 27th 1938. Naming ceremony by H.M. Queen Elizabeth.

their legs. 1Lt Pohlman suggested that he and Weed buy some soft drinks and snacks for the men of F Company from a fund that they had for such things. Pohlman and Weed went into the depot and bargained for some drinks and food. About the time, they came back to the train with armloads of candy bars and drinks, the train started to pull away from the station. They were immediately assured that the train was only going down the tracks for some short ways to get some water. But, the train kept going and Pohlman and Weed had to hop another train to catch up to their unit.(1.)

Camp Kilmer, New Jersey was a staging post for troops leaving for Europe. At that time of year, it was a hot, sweltering place with few accommodations and Spartan living conditions. Soon after arriving at Camp Kilmer, Lt. Weed invited a few of the other lieutenants to come with him to New York City for the weekend and stay at his family's suite at the Waldorf Astoria Hotel. Weed, Berry, Ellis, 2Lt Withers from F Company and 2Lt Buckner from E Company went along with several others.

They mostly spent their time resting and eating and exploring a few blocks immediately around the hotel. Although they could have obtained tickets to a Brooklyn Dodgers game or had some fun at nearby Coney Island, they mostly just hung around the hotel and enjoyed some quiet time away from their units.

For a few days at Camp Kilmer, the officers of the 19th Engineer Regiment worked to train their men and to check equipment and gear. The Regiment spent about a month in the hot "oven" called Camp Kilmer and in mid-August 1942, the unit was assigned to II Corps commanded by Major General Fredendall and was ordered to report to the harbor in New York City for embarkation.

The 19th loaded onto trains at Camp Kilmer and rode the rails for a few short miles to the docks at New York City. Upon arrival, they were surprised to see what they thought was the biggest ship in the world! Indeed, it was. They would be crammed into the brand-new HMS Queen Elizabeth and take its first voyage east across the Atlantic. After loading men, supplies, vehicles and equipment for several days, the huge ship pulled away from the dock toward their eastern destination. An airplane escorted the ship out to sea, but before long, they were alone in the Atlantic. Jerry remembers asking why the ship wasn't zigzagging. Everyone was aware that Nazi submarines lurked below the Atlantic waiting for such a great prize to sink. He was told by one of the crew that the Queen Elizabeth was faster than any submarine and therefore there was no need to zigzag.

On the way over the Atlantic, officers were assigned to state rooms which were gradually being reconstructed to hold troop units. There were several thousand carpenters on board the ship and you could hear saws, hammers and drills constantly during the voyage. Senior officers were assigned to state rooms that had been finished and were furnished with beds and furniture. Jerry and the other three lieutenants of F Company shared a small state room and slept on cots.

Their accommodations, however, were much better than their men. Men slept in shifts in cots or hammocks stacked as much as 6-high, deep in the bowels of the ship. There were around 17,000 soldiers on the ship.(1.) Days were spent with as much time as possible on deck performing military training as well as they could on the crowded ship. They, of course, had no idea where they were headed but it seemed obvious that they were headed to Great Britain.

Meanwhile, elsewhere in the war, the German Luftwaffe was decimating a convoy to relieve the English protectorate of Malta in the Mediterranean and the German army was continuing to advance toward Stalingrad in Russia. In Washington, DC, General George S. Patton and well as Jimmy Dootittle and others meet in to plan Operation Torch, the invasion of North Africa by the Allies.

As the HMS Queen Elizabeth is nearing Scotland, the Battle of Alam Halfa is raging in Egypt. It is the last attempt by Rommel to break through the Allied lines in Egypt and to take Cairo and the Suez Canal. The Allied victory in the Battle is the beginning of the end for the Afrika Corps but they still have a lot of fight left in them as the 19th Engineers will find out in a few months at the Battle of Kasserine Pass.

*A British Valentine tank in North Africa, perhaps during the Battle of Alam Halfa.*

# Great Britain

After several days at sea the nervous troops were very glad to see land approach. The HMS Queen Elizabeth landed at Greenock, Scotland August 31, 1942, with no serious incident. Greenock is the port city for Glasgow. As they sailed into port, the men could see ships everywhere. It was a busy harbor and there were dozens of barrage balloons held by cables all around the city.

As Berry was, alphabetically, the first 2d Lieutenant, he was assigned to check people off as they came down the gangplank, which, of course, meant that he was the last of the Regiment to get off of the ship and to get to chow. The men were directed to a tent city in Greenock where they ate and relaxed for a few hours. After a quick meal, the 19th loaded onto a smaller ship, the Princess Maud and set sail to Ireland.

(1.)

*The ship Princes Maud, circa 1941.*

The Princess Maude looked like a toy beside the Queen Elizabeth. It had been one of the ships that had taken part in the evacuation of Dunkirk in 1940 after the fall of France. Bullet holes from German strafing could be seen all over her sides. The 19th spent an uncomfortable night on The Princess Maud, and looked forward to finding themselves on land for a while. On the ship, they exchanged money for Irish pounds. They landed at the Bay of Belfast the next morning, on September 1, 1942.(1.)

When they first arrived, a black quartermaster unit was already on site preparing for arrival of the Americans. There were American trucks waiting for them as well. They were assigned trucks and drove to an estate about two hours from Belfast near the town of Antrim where they bivouacked. Field grade officers stayed in the mansion while the troops stayed in Quonset huts which had been previously erected on the grounds in the middle of an apple orchard.

Around 30 men lived in each Quonset hut. They stayed in this location for about 1½ months. While there, the weather was rainy and cool almost every day as fall approached Northern Ireland. During off hours, the men played cards, wrote letters home and tried to follow the results of the ongoing war in Africa and Russia.

On September 16, 1941, he wrote a "V-mail" home to Mary Frances, as follows: *"Hello Darling: No excitement at all today – got 3 more of your letters – you're wonderful! I've been awfully busy. This camp is in the worst of conditions – everything is wrong. If it doesn't stop raining, I'll go nuts – it continually rains and rains. Incidentally, how is school? You'll be just starting when you receive this – won't that slow you down? – Reading these terribly long letters – Ha! How is the V-Mail letters? If they arrive as fast as regular air mail, let me know! Betcha your sorority is getting the cream of the cop. I hope so anyway. Good luck, Fran, and do be careful & always remember to – Love, Jerry."*

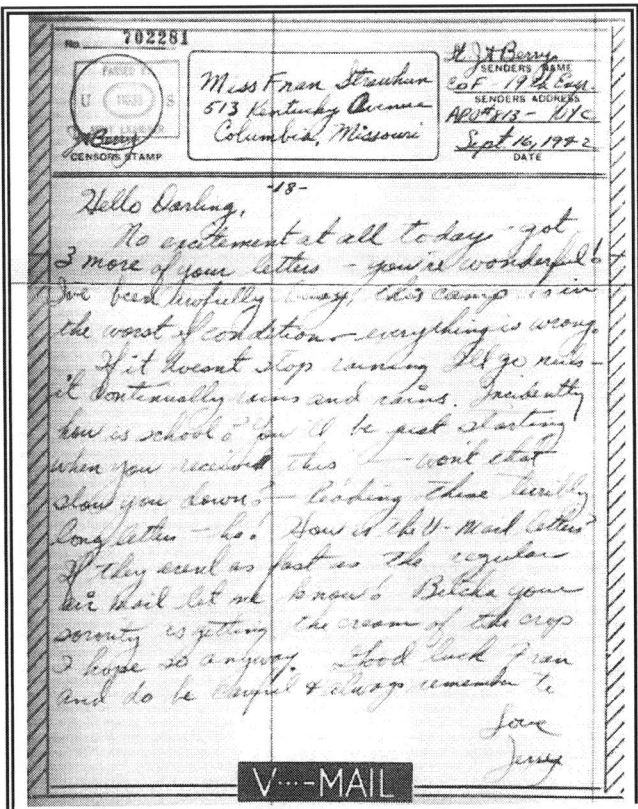

*2Lt Berry sent this "V-mail" letter to Mary Francis Strawhun on September 16, 1942, a couple of weeks after arriving in Great Britain.*

The 19th had little to do while in Antrim. The regiment was issued weapons while there. Officers were issued .45 caliber pistols while enlisted men were issued M1 rifles. There was a small rifle range nearby and the men spent quite a lot of time working on marksmanship and getting used to their new "best friend". They also trained on first aid, map reading and other subjects until mid-October 1942.

On a few occasions, some of the lieutenants were able to get to Belfast for a few hours. Jerry was able to get away and stayed at the Grand Central Hotel for a night on September 19.

*Typical Quonset hut installation c. 1941.*

The IRA was active in Northern Ireland at that time. They did not like Americans because the US had joined sides with the British. The IRA was considered dangerous to the American troops located there. When soldiers went to the town of Antrim, they were required to go in groups of at least four in order to

*Cave Hill and Belfast Castle, Northern Ireland.*

minimize their danger. There were several hotels, dance halls and pubs in Antrim. There were always a number of local girls in the dance halls that were ready to dance with the Americans. Lt Berry went to town on several occasions but most of the time was spent attending to business. Merle Oberon, an American movie star of the 1940's, came to Belfast on one occasion as part of a USO show. She and her entourage had a reception in town but only Colonels were able to see her.

In mid-October, the 19th was ordered to relocate to Southern England and Lts Ellis and Berry were assigned to the advance party, composed of around 20 troops. The advance party was ordered to prepare an area in England to house the remainder of the 2d Battalion of the 19th Engineers. They loaded into boats and crossed the Irish Sea to the west coast of England, to the city of Chester. From Chester, they drove to Oulton Park[1], England, about 6 miles from Chester, to an estate where English commandos had recently bivouacked. There, the advanced party of the 19th settled into an area of Quonset huts which had been erected for the commandos and began preparations for the arrival of the rest of the battalion. This is where Lt Berry got the nickname of "Old Bob."

---

[1] The author could not find any place near Chester that is named Oulton Park.

Lt Berry and the rest of the advanced party gathered supplies such as toilet paper, fuel, ammunition, rations, etc. Jerry still recalls drawing toilet paper rations from the British who allotted only four squares of paper per soldier per day.

At the camp, there was a large supply of 5-gallon cans of gasoline. Because it was so valuable, they had to guard the gasoline constantly. The first night that they arrived at the camp, Lt Berry was assigned as the officer in charge of the guard. One of his platoon members, Pvt. Hewlett, was standing guard at the fuel dump and Berry told him to watch for people trying to steal the gasoline. He told him that if he saw anyone approach the fuel dump, to not fire at the person under any circumstances but to fire three times in the air in order to scare off the would-be thief.

Soon after Jerry went to bed, just about dawn, a local thug needing gasoline and carrying a fuel can, snuck

When I'm sitting alone and dreaming
Of the days that used to be,
My heart goes back in fancy
To the old home by the sea.
Copyright.

SHEEP ISLAND, ANTRIM COAST ROAD.
7232

up to the area where the fuel was stored. Sure enough, just as he was told to do, Hewlett yelled "Halt!" and then fired three times in the air and the smuggler took off. Jerry jumped up from his cot and went running toward the fuel dump to see what was happening. Pvt. Hewlett was there, pretty upset as he had never fired near another person. Pvt. Hewlett said that he thought the would-be thief was still nearby hiding in the bushes. Jerry told Hewlett to empty his M-1 in the air in the direction of the thief to scare him away, which he did.

As the smuggler ran off, Hewlett and Berry settled back in as the morning approached. Just after dawn, a local farmer came walking up to Berry and Hewlett shaking his finger at them and obviously mad. As he approached, he said, "I say, you've killed my horse." He went on to say that he had heard shots as he was getting out of bed and that when he went out to his farm yard, his horse was standing in the yard bleeding to death with a bullet hole in his breast.

Jerry went with the farmer up to his farm to see for himself. When they got there, the farmer showed Jerry the horse with a bullet hole in his breast, standing in a pool of blood. About that time, the veterinarian showed up and determined that it was too late for the horse so he shot him in the head. Then the vet asked, "Where's Old Bob?" The farmer said that he didn't know and the three of them went looking for the farmer's other horse, "Old Bob". Soon they saw Old Bob lying on the ground, shot in the lower leg. The vet determined that there was no way to save Old Bob, so Jerry watched in horror as the vet shot Old Bob, too.

After the ruckus, Jerry returned to camp and reported to LTC. Kellogg that the 19th had accidentally killed two horses. Soon, a group of citizens came to the camp and told Jerry that he had to appear before a local magistrate in Chester at 9:00 that morning. So, LTC. Kellogg and Lt Berry took off in a jeep to attend court in Chester. Upon arrival, the magistrate was there in his full regalia, white wig and all. LTC. Kellogg assured the magistrate that the US government would pay for the two horses which seemed to appease all concerned. Jerry later went and visited the farmer and gave him some rations. During that visit, it was discovered that the family were Methodists and Jerry explained that he was a Methodist, also, which caused the family to befriend Berry. He ended up attending church services with the family several times and enjoyed their companionship while he was stationed at Oulton Park.

For the rest of the war, Jerry was jokingly called "Old Bob" by members of F Company.

During the war, Jerry and the Oulton Park family exchanged letters several times. Decades later during a tour of England, Jerry and his wife, Mary Frances, went looking for the Oulton Park area and the church. He found out that the mansion had been turned into a restaurant.

*This photo is, perhaps, of the family in England that befriended Lt Berry. It was found in his belongings after he died in July 2005.*

Later, when LTC. Kellogg, the battalion commander arrived, he and Lt Berry and Lt Ellis, were invited to the mansion for a reception in honor of the newly arrived American advance party. The three officers scoured for a clean uniform, got all of their brass on and got ready for the reception just as it began to rain. The three officers got in a jeep with the top down and drove to the mansion in the pouring rain. Soon after they arrived they were escorted, dripping wet, to the mansion by a servant.

Later that evening, LTC. Kellogg approached Berry and whispered in his ear that he had to go back to their camp area and bring some toilet paper to the estate, as there was none in the mansion. Although the TP was a very precious commodity to the Americans, Berry did as he was ordered and went back to camp, took two rolls, put them under his raincoat, and drove back to the mansion. When he got back, he ran out of the rain into the mansion when, just then, a roll of TP fell out from under his coat and rolled across the room much to the embarrassment of all present. Lt Berry was kidded about that incident throughout the war. However, during the next 3 years, the story seemed to grow as it was re-told so that eventually the story grew so that several rolls fell out.

The rest of the 19th never did arrive in Oulton Park. By late-October, as the advance party was finalizing the arrangements for the 19th's arrival, the 19th was diverted to Liverpool. After a few more days in Oulton Park, the advance party was ordered to meet the rest of the regiment near Liverpool. So, the advance party, including Berry, Ellis and LTC. Kellogg, along with all of the gear and equipment of the advance party, hopped on a train in Chester and rode the rails to Liverpool.

On October 20, 1942, the men were told that they were loading onto a ship at Greenock. They were to load onto trucks at 1800 hours and convoy to the harbor at Greenock. Weed, Ellis and Berry got to the loading area at 1730 and decided to have an ale while they waited. The ale went down pretty easily and pretty fast which beckoned another. Soon the three of them had had several ales and when the trucks were late, more ale was ordered. They were soon joined by other men as they arrived and pretty soon the ale was pouring like water. By the time the trucks arrived, the three lieutenants were all ready for a nap in the nice warm truck cabs which they enjoyed all the way to Greenock.(1.)

The next morning the 19th loaded onto troop ships. There were hundreds of ships in the harbor all in various stages of loading equipment and soldiers. Large cranes were loading vehicles, including tanks, onto ships. Large bales of C rations and other supplies were being hoisted and lowered in ship hulls. Men were assembling and filing single file up gang planks under the watchful eyes of non-commissioned officers. Gradually, the men and supplies of the 19th were loaded and their ship pulled out of Greenock harbor on a cold, windy, sleety day around October 25th. Berry and his unit were on the USS Washington (1.).

*The battleship USS Washington, launched, 1940.*

There were many other ships in their convoy filled with soldiers, sailors and equipment. Their convoy included at least a hundred ships with naval vessels on the perimeter of the convoy to protect the troop ships. The men were packed tightly in their ships with little to do and no room to do it. Each morning Jerry led F Company in calisthenics that he called "the football exercise" that quickly took a toll on the men.(1.) They tried to train and pass the time constructively but without a lot of luck.

Unknown to them, they were to be in the first wave of the invasion of North Africa. During the last year, the Allied high command had been planning what was to be the largest invasion by sea in the history of the world. The men of the 19th were destined to be part of it.

# North Africa

Several other units were on the ship but no one seemed to know where they were going or why. Each morning, because alphabetically, he was the first 2d lieutenant, Berry lead the troops in calisthenics. Every night they listened to the BBC news reports which were nearly all bad news about Allied losses in Russia and Egypt.

Troops slept in hammocks piled 5-6 high throughout the ship. Many of the men slept on the deck to avoid the close quarters of the sleeping area. They trained during the day by doing close order drill, marksmanship practice, and cleaning weapons. They also trained climbing the nets along the side of the ships with full gear.

After several nights on board, they woke up one morning to see hundreds of other ships and airplanes. According to Jerry, "as far as you could see, there were ships heading in the same direction." Ships employed large balloons fastened by cable to the ships as anti-strafing devises, which the troops liked to use as shooting targets. They were warned several times not to shoot at the balloons, but it was too much temptation for some of the troops.

*Field Marshall Kesselring and Field Marshall Rommel, 1943.(10.)*

*Lt. Berry in North Africa, 1943.*

Finally, around November 6th, the officers were called together and were briefed on the pending invasion. They were all told that they were going to land in Algeria but that there would be no resistance as the Allies were negotiating with the Vichy French to not fight the Americans. They were also told that they were going to land at 0100 hours (1:00 in the morning), which made them all wonder why they were going to land at that time if there was not going to be any resistance.

During the days on board, the troops practiced climbing rope ladders and getting into "landing craft". Most of the landing craft were nothing more than rubber rafts with a plywood floor. Most of the rubber rafts were old and had not been maintained.

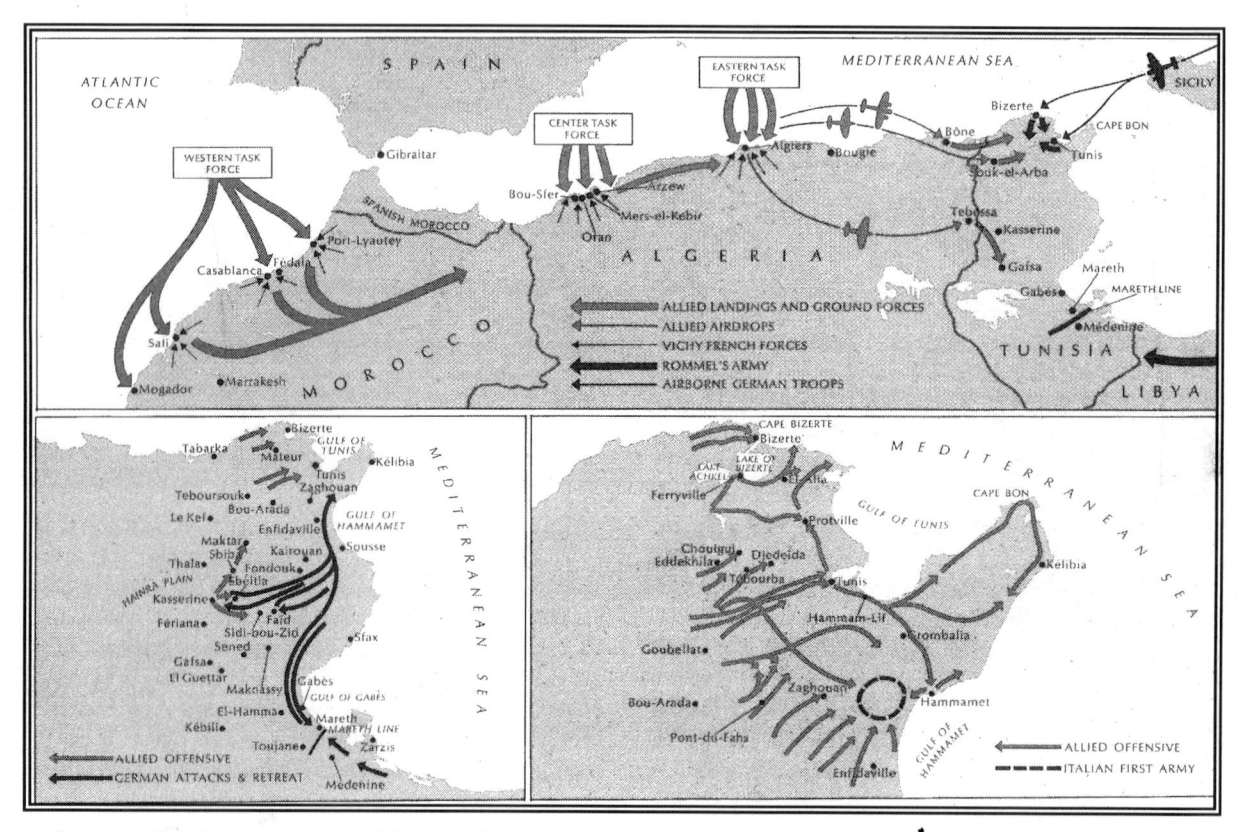

*Operation Torch was composed of three simultaneous landings of Allied forces. In the west, General Patton lead forces landing at four places in Morocco; in the center, where the 19th Engineers were landing Gen Fredendall commanded, American and British forces landed at Oran; and, in the East, American and British forces landed in and around Algiers.*

As yet, no American had died in battle. No mothers had lost sons; no wives had lost husbands; no child had lost a father. The men on board the many ships heading for the northern beaches of Africa had been trained but none had seen combat. Very few knew where they were going or what awaited them. Over 70,000 of them would die during the next few weeks at places they could hardly pronounce, like Faid Pass, Sidi Nsir, Bizerte, Oran, El Guettar, Kasserine Pass, Casablanca and Hill 609. They would become wounded or maimed or killed in countries that few could point to on a map. They would fight and die to liberate countries made up largely of deserts of sand and mountains of rock.

North Africa would soon be the testing ground for the great commanders of World War II: Rommel, Montgomery, Patton, Eisenhower, Truscott, Clark and Bradley. North Africa is where the Allies began to beat back the "invincible" German Army. North Africa is where tank war fare came of age. North Africa was the place where the first of 2 million Americans would first fight the Germans. Planning for the invasion of North Africa, Operation Torch, had begun.

# Allied Chain of Command

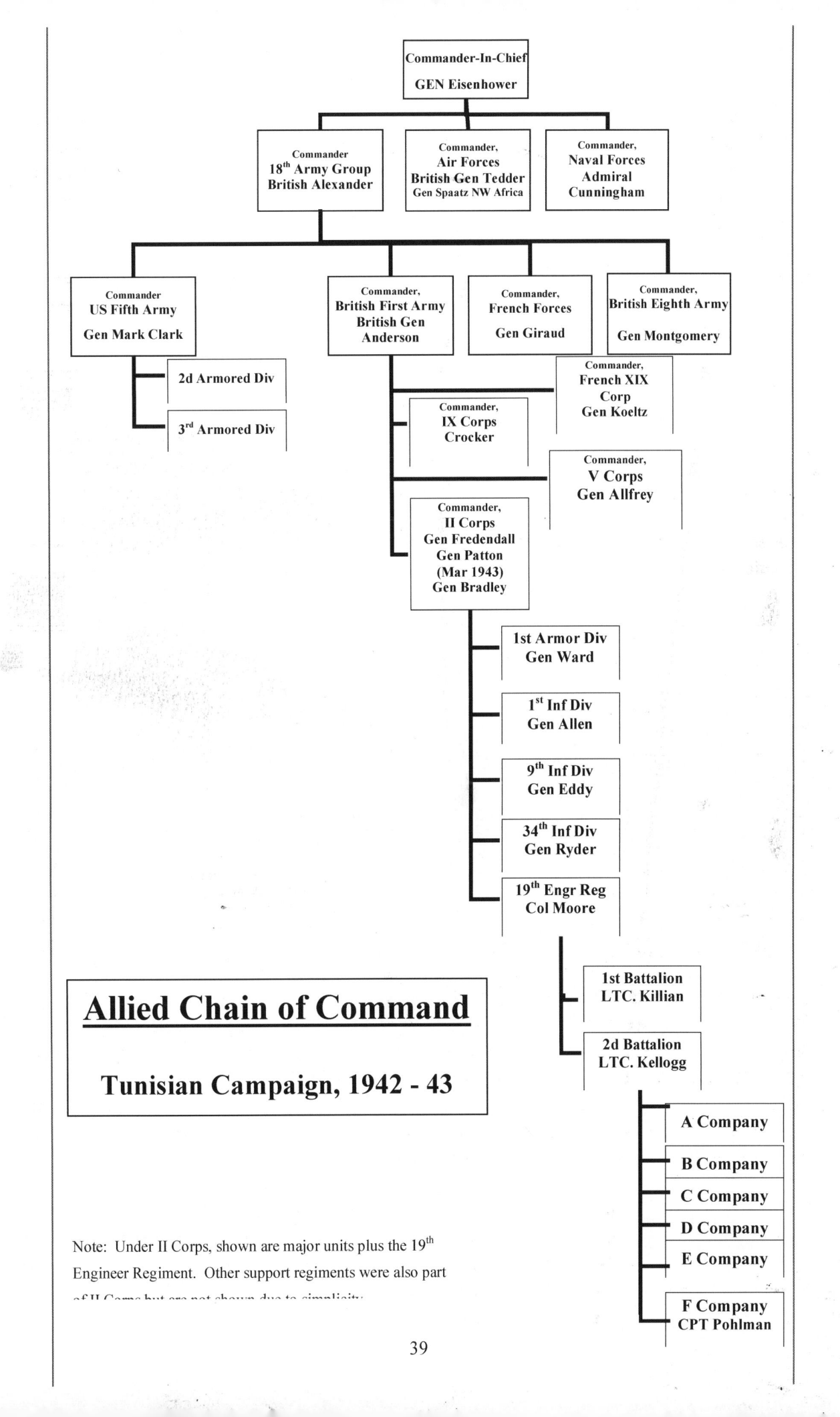

## Tunisian Campaign, 1942 - 43

- **Commander-In-Chief** — GEN Eisenhower
  - **Commander 18th Army Group** — British Alexander
    - **Commander US Fifth Army** — Gen Mark Clark
      - 2d Armored Div
      - 3rd Armored Div
    - **Commander, British First Army** — British Gen Anderson
      - **Commander, IX Corps** — Crocker
      - **Commander, V Corps** — Gen Allfrey
      - **Commander, II Corps** — Gen Fredendall / Gen Patton (Mar 1943) / Gen Bradley
        - 1st Armor Div — Gen Ward
        - 1st Inf Div — Gen Allen
        - 9th Inf Div — Gen Eddy
        - 34th Inf Div — Gen Ryder
        - 19th Engr Reg — Col Moore
          - 1st Battalion — LTC. Killian
          - 2d Battalion — LTC. Kellogg
            - A Company
            - B Company
            - C Company
            - D Company
            - E Company
            - F Company — CPT Pohlman
    - **Commander, French Forces** — Gen Giraud
      - **Commander, French XIX Corp** — Gen Koeltz
    - **Commander, British Eighth Army** — Gen Montgomery
  - **Commander, Air Forces** — British Gen Tedder / Gen Spaatz NW Africa
  - **Commander, Naval Forces** — Admiral Cunningham

Note: Under II Corps, shown are major units plus the 19th Engineer Regiment. Other support regiments were also part of II Corps but are not shown due to simplicity.

# Operation Torch

Now that Roosevelt had ordered the invasion of North Africa as the first confrontation with Germany since Dunkirk, plans for Operation Torch began to be formed. In August 1942, Roosevelt was convinced by his staff that if the British came ashore simultaneously with the Americans, that the French who would be defending Morocco, Algeria and Tunisia, would most definitely fight due to their hatred of the British. However, U.S. military staff believed that if the first wave of men ashore were all Americans that the French would likely not fight and would surrender immediately. Then, it was reasoned, the British could follow in the second wave ashore. In September 1941, Churchill agreed and the invasion forces began to take shape.

The next question was where to land. It was believed by most that it was critical to control Tunisia within two weeks of the landing in order to prevent the Germans and Italians from reinforcing their forces from Italy. Once Tunisia was seized, Allied control of the Mediterranean was all but assured. Rommel's Afrika Korps would be trapped in Libya with the British Eight Army under Montgomery to their east in Egypt and the Americans to their west in Tunisia. At that point, the allies would also control a springboard to Sicily and Italy.

Various plans were drawn for locations of the landings. It was considered that Axis air power could cause havoc from bases in Sicily and Italy if troops landed in Tunisia. The further west the landings took place, the farther they would be from Germany's air support. Arguments and debates followed as the American and British strategists took all possibilities into account.

*General Nogues (left) commander of French Morocco and Maj Gen George S. Patton just after the armistice between Vichy France and the Allies in Rabat, Morocco.*

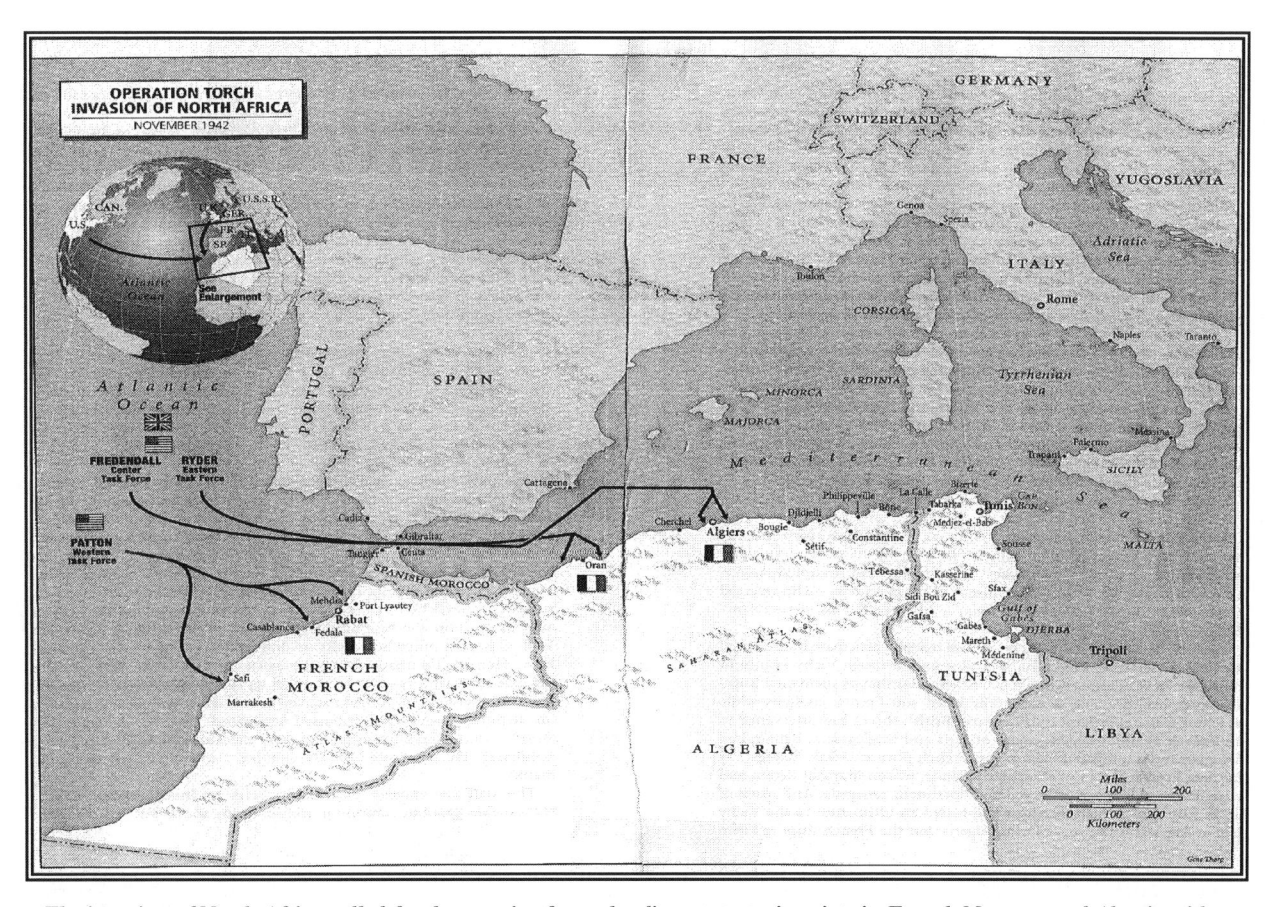

*The invasion of North Africa called for three major forces landing at strategic points in French Morocco and Algeria with an immediate drive to the east to take Tunisia and to trap the Germans in Libya. Patton led the western task force landing in French Morocco. Fredendall, commander of II Corps, lead the center task force landing around Oran. General Ryder commanded the eastern task force landing around Algiers. As part of II Corps, the 19th Engineers landed with the center task force around Oran. The Allies hoped for light resistance from the Vichy French forces defending Morocco and Algeria. (2.)*

Finally, on September 5, 1942, the decision was made to land at three sites in Morocco and six different locations around Algiers and Oran. On September 21st, Eisenhower set the date for the landings for Sunday morning, November 8, 1942. The plan called for 300 warships and nearly 400 transports and cargo vessels to land more than 100,000 troops, 75% of them American, in North Africa. The hope was that the Vichy French would not fight. Regardless, as soon as the landings took place, all units would turn east and drive ferociously toward Tunis.

General George S. Patton was chosen to lead the Western Task Force which was to land from the Atlantic on the shores of Morocco with three divisions: the 9th Infantry, the 3rd Infantry and the 2nd Armor divisions. Supplies, ammunition, gasoline, blood plasma, weapons, artillery, vehicles, medical equipment, rations, and 34,000 troops were loaded on the largest fleet to ever sail from American waters by October 24th. On the morning of October 25, 1942, Patton and his task force sailed from Norfolk, Virginia to rendezvous with the rest of the invasion fleet across the Atlantic.

General Fredendall, commander of II Corps, was the commander of the center task force which was to land in Algeria and take the important port of Oran. General Ryder commanded the eastern task force planned to land around and to take Algiers, the capital of Algeria and an important port as well as the closest landing place to Tunisia. Both of these task forces were to leave from several different ports in Great Britain.

Ships were loaded in Britain with tens of thousands of tons of war supplies including barber chairs, hand tools to be used by native Algerians and 390,000 pairs of socks. Also included were 72,000 American and British troops, about two thirds of whom were Americans. The troops were part of the US 1st Infantry Division commanded by General Terry Allen, the 1st Armored Division and the 34th Infantry Division as well as a number of regiments, including the 19th Engineer Regiment commanded by Colonel ATW Moore. British troops sewed American flags on their sleeves so that the Vichy French would be less likely to fire on them.

By October 25th the troops and supplies were loaded and the two task forces were sailing for their rendezvous with Patton's western task force and their fate in North Africa. General Theodore Roosevelt, assistant commander of the 1st Infantry Division and son of President Teddy Roosevelt, wrote his wife on October 26th, "Here I am off again on the great adventure."

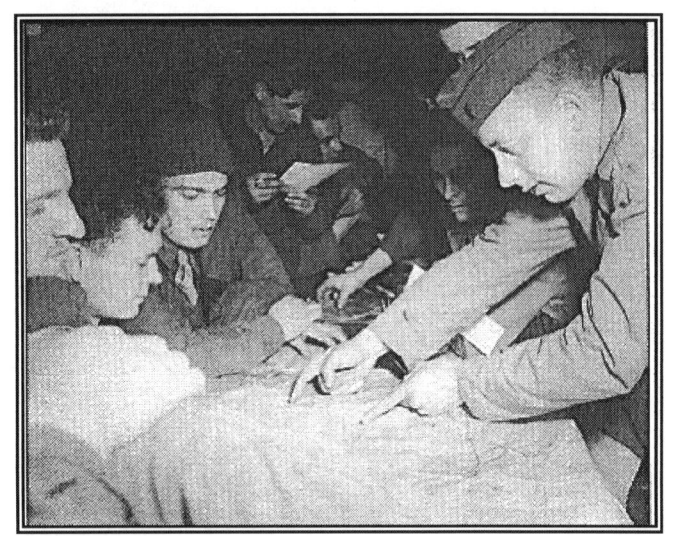

*Men from the 1st Ranger Battalion review a map of Arzew aboard ship just hours before landing. (2.)*

Morale wasn't as good with the men below the waterline. Bunks were stacked as much as 6 high. There was little room to move and there was a stench of sweat, oil and woolen blankets along with the air from hundreds of men in close quarters. Much of the food that was served was fatty mutton and the bread was full of insects and weevils. Men washed mess kits with sea water which caused dysentery. There were long lines at the dispensaries for men who were sea sick or sick from the food or sick from dysentery or just, plain sick.

Shortly after sunset on November 5, 1942, the convoy turned east at the Straits of Gibraltar and entered the Mediterranean. Soon after, the fleet split into two forces: task force center, with 39,000 men headed for Oran; and, task force east, with 33,000 men headed for Algiers. The 19th Engineers, as part of the center task force, was around General Roosevelt when he wrote his wife, "The die is cast, and the result is on the knees of God."

By then, General Eisenhower had landed in Gibraltar where the command headquarters hurried with last minute details and mostly, worried. While Eisenhower was setting up shop on Gibraltar, General Mark Clark was setting ashore from a submarine to meet secretly with Vichy French officers who were ready to surrender to the Americans. All looked ready for an easy victory in North Africa. Instead, the French forces in North Africa did fight!

The invasion of North Africa marked the first fighting by American units in World War II. On November 8, 1942, Allied forces landed all across North Africa from Morocco to Algeiers. Oran, Algeria was a major port in a critical area of the Mediterranean and was the primary objective of the Allied invasion. Defending the Algerian coast were the Vichy French with the German Army under Rommel, east of Algeria fighting the British under Montgomery.

*Lt Berry's weapon's platoon in North Africa, November 1943. Front row, left to right: Pvt Marticheski (with machine gun), Tec4 John Mata, Tec4 Justin Merriman, Pvt Peterson; Standing, back row, left to right: Sgt Fred Theiss, Pvt Arthur Wing, Pvt Julius Wagner, Pvt Joe Boxley, Tec4 Lenny Levetsky and Pvt John Sckorupski, with machine gun.*

*The Port of Oran, Algeria, c. 1942*

*The Port of Arzew, Algeria, near Oran, c. 1942.*

*The Company F logo was designed by Cpl Frank Pikrone of Chicago and was painted on most of the company's vehicles. It shows Donald Duck with a whiskey bottle in hand peering through the letter F.*

The center task force was commanded by Major General Lloyd Fredendall and was further split into three forces with the objective of capturing Oran with its ports intact and in good condition in order to use the facilities for off-loading troops and equipment in later waves. General Theodore Roosevelt commanded the troops ordered to land on Beaches X and Y to the west of Oran.

*The 1st Rangers capture a French gun emplacement at Arzew, east of Oran, November 8, 1942. (2.)*

Major General Terry Allen commanded the troops ordered to land to the east of Oran on Beach Z near Arzew, 16 miles to the east of Oran. Major General Orlando Ward commanded the 1st Armored Division which provided the troops for the assault on the port of Oran itself with the intent to taking it intact. The assault on Oran was spearheaded by the 3$^{rd}$ Battalion of the 6$^{th}$ Armored Infantry Regiment, an element of the 1$^{st}$ Armored Division.

The plan was for the center force to capture the facilities of the Port of Oran while the two forces east and west of Oran drove toward Oran in a pinching move.

At 12:01 AM, the crews took battle stations, scrambling nets were thrown over the side and the men of the center assault, called Operation Reservist, went over the side and made way to Oran. As the men neared Oran, machine gun fire erupted from Oran. Soon heavier fire poured on the cutters which were off-loading the assault forces.

Landing boats capsized and explosions destroyed parts of the cutters. The assault forces took heavy casualties as they swept ashore. The Vichy French were, indeed fighting! As assault forces grappled to shore, they were mowed down by waiting French forces. Casualties of Operation Reservist topped 90%, about half of whom were killed. French marines rounded up survivors and took them to a prison.

Meanwhile, ships were sunk in the harbor and floating docks were destroyed to keep the Allies from using them. Corpses of Americans and British troops bobbed to the surface for weeks to come. There were more than 300 dead to start the first American assault on Axis forces. Meanwhile, troops were landing on Beaches X, Y and Z. The largest force landed at Beach Z near Arzew under the command of General Allen. Elements of the 1st Rangers were to storm the two fortresses nearest to Arzew.

Just before 1:00 AM, naval batteries started the bombardment of the beaches while airplanes could be heard overhead strafing and bombing Vichy French positions on the beaches. Simultaneously, the Vichy French shore batteries started their fire at the Allies.

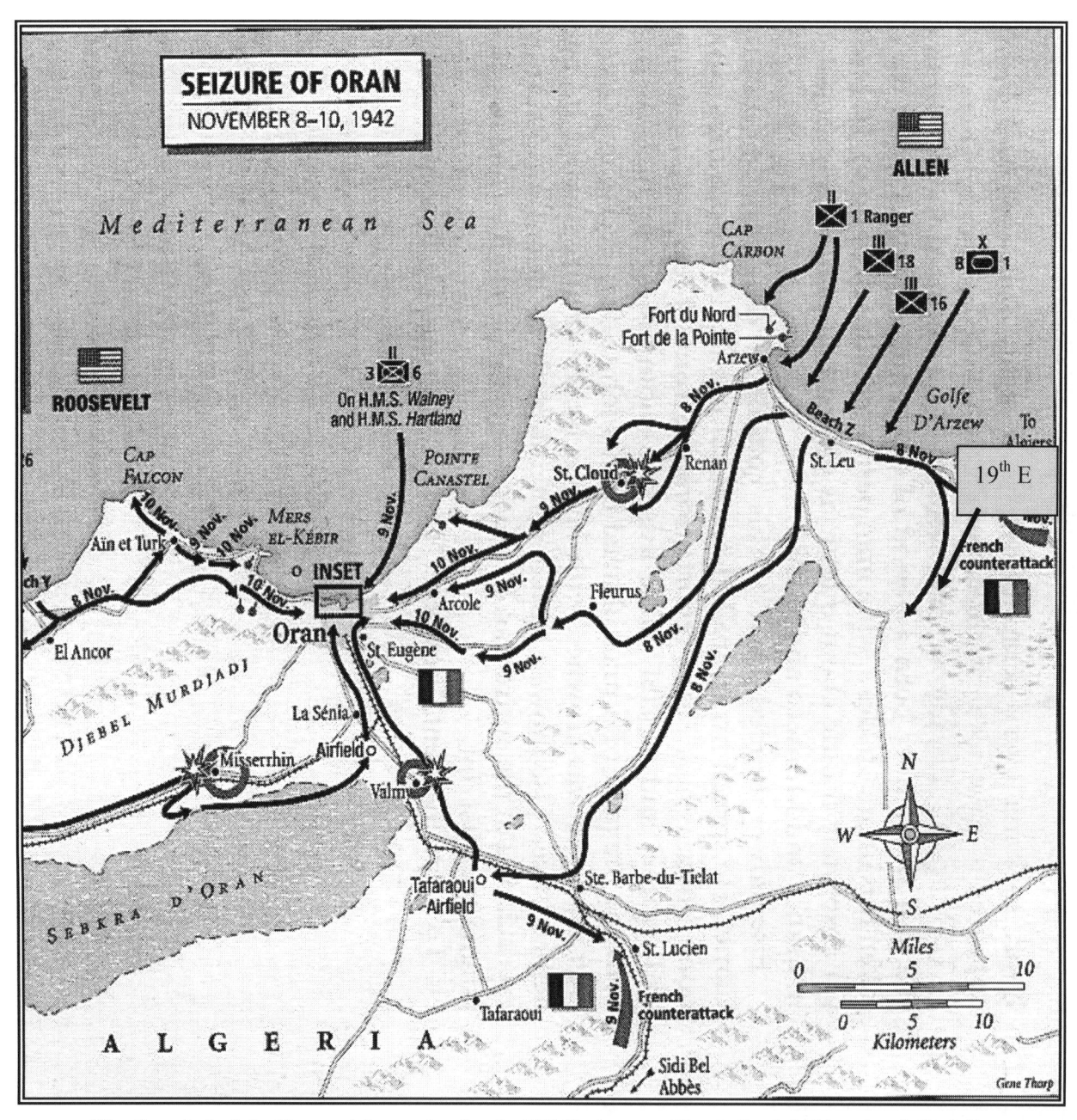

*The plan of attack for Oran and Arzew, showing the 19th Engineer position to the right (American's far left).*

Allen's forces that landed on Beach Z, in addition to the Rangers, were composed of a regiment of the 18th Infantry Division, a regiment of the 16th Infantry Division, a Brigade of the 1st Armored Division and elements of the 19th Engineer Regiment, which included 2Lt Berry and his weapons platoon.

The 19th was split into several different landing waves. Some of the 19th, including Berry and his weapons platoon, landed in the first wave with other units split between other waves over a three day period.

As the men assigned to Beach Z were scrambling down nets to the assault boats below, chaos awaited them on the beach. For the invasion, Jerry was assigned to the first wave as commander of the F Company weapons platoon of about 32 men. He ordered the platoon into three boats, about 10-11 men per raft. Getting into the rubber rafts was very difficult for the troops. Each man was loaded with gear and climbed down a rope ladder at least 50 feet to the awaiting raft. The rafts, however, were rising and falling many feet as the waves passed making it nearly impossible to judge how far the bottom of the raft was from your feet. As a soldier would step into the raft, the raft would suddenly drop 5 feet and the soldier, along with his gear, would fall into the raft, or, worse, into the water. Several rafts were damaged that way and lots of equipment and a few men of the Allied force were lost.

In addition, westerly winds had caused the boats to land off course and many of the coxswains were

*US troops come ashore near Oran, Algeria on November 8, 1942. In the foreground is probably the same railroad track that Lt. Berry's weapons platoon re-conned for 3 days.(8.)*

confused in the dark of the night. Soon they were all loaded and away they went, in the dark with fire all around, bullets flying, and artillery shells landing in the water nearby.

Berry's platoon got loaded and took off with paddles frantically paddling toward the waiting beach and the "friendly Vichy French" who were firing everything that they had at them. As they approached the beaches, the French poured fire onto the troops. One American battalion commander yelled, "Okay, boys it's open season, fire at will."

*This railroad track near Bizerte, Tunisia must be similar to the one Berry's Weapons Platoon re-conned on November 8, 9 and 10, 1942.*

The rafts were designed, supposedly, in compartments so that if a bullet went through one compartment, the other compartments would be able to keep the raft afloat. This information proved to be about as accurate as the briefing that said the Vichy French would not fight. About 200 yards from the ship, Berry's raft was hit by shrapnel or rifle fire and quickly sank.

The troops on the raft were soon floundering in the Mediterranean with life jackets on and holding their gear and their weapons. Each man had nearly 100 pounds of gear that weighed them down and made it very difficult to maneuver. Shortly, British commandos came by in another boat so Berry's troops hung on to the side of the commando's raft as they paddled to shore. However, when the American's raft sank, most of the unit's rations, ammo and gear, sank with it.

Soon, the raft approached shore and the troops were able to wade to the beach. The platoon landed on the far-left flank of Beach Z, and was the furthest unit east of Arzew.

Berry immediately found his platoon and gathered them, ready for action. Just about the time the platoon was assembled, General Allen, appeared out of nowhere and walked up to Berry and said, "I'm General Allen, what unit are you with?" Berry told him that he was platoon leader of the weapons platoon of F Company, 2d battalion, 19th Combat Engineers. General Allen pulled out a map and a small pen light and showed Berry the map. He pointed out where they were and said "see this railroad track?" He said, "I want you to take your platoon east along this

*1st Rangers on Arzew beach, November 8, 1942. (14.)*

48

railroad track until you meet resistance and then hang on until we reinforce you.

Berry's weapons platoon were armed with three machine guns and M-1 rifles but little else and little ammunition. They had no rations and little water, and no blankets or other gear.

So, off they went, around 2:00 AM heading east in the dark, down a railroad track in the desert of Algeria, looking for Germans or Vichy French. All were pretty scared and, at first, were very careful while they advanced. Behind them they could hear small arms fire, machine guns, mortar shells and artillery pounding both lines. Flares filled the skies and airplanes bombed and strafed the entrenched Vichy French to their rear. According to Jerry, "there was a Hellova war going on behind us."

*2Lt Berry meeting with Algerians near Arzew shortly after landing, November 1942. It looks like he is trading candy for some Algerian souvenirs. He has a pipe in his left hand.*

But on they went, Berry's weapons' platoon, looking for a fight with Rommel or the French, whichever they encountered first. They used infantry tactics as they advanced, crawling and covering each other as they advanced in the night. Yet, the further they went, the further away the war seemed to be. But, orders from a General are nothing to sneeze at so they trudged on and gradually became a little lazier and a little less tactical. Finally, dawn arrived and they had not yet seen or heard another soul, Germans, Vichy French, or anybody else.

On they went, all day on November 8th until they finally stopped to rest that night. They had nothing to eat and very little water and no other gear to make camp. Nearby a donkey "hee-hawed" several times and Berry thought it was a "wild animal in North Africa". Some of his troops kidded him because he didn't know the sound of a donkey.
November 8th was full of confusion, valor, death and victory. The French fought and killed and died. Near Arzew, some troops heard a tank clanking down the street in the dark. All of the men opened fire only to find an Algerian with a donkey and a cart with a tank of wine full of bullet holes. Allen's 18th

Infantry Regiment pressed the attack westerly toward St. Cloud and Oran while the 16th pressed southwest on the 18th 's left flank. 1st Armor headed southwest toward Ste. Barbe-du-Tielat with little resistance.

Around noon on November 8th, the two columns pressed toward Oran and continued to advance. From Beach Z, General Allen's 1st Infantry Division descended on Oran from the sandstone hills above St. Cloud, which was a key crossroads east of the city. Facing the 1st Division at St. Cloud were the 16th Tunisian Infantry Regiment, the 1st Battalion of the French Foreign Legion, an artillery battalion and local paramilitary troops. The French ambushed leading elements of the American 1st Infantry and drove them back. As they returned with reinforcements, they were driven back again. At 3:30 PM the 1st Infantry attacked again and managed to out flank them and fierce fighting continued as the 1st advanced into St. Cloud. (2.)

As night fell, men were lying in any place of shelter that they could find with dead bodies of their comrades all around them. At 7:00 AM on the 9th, the attack was resumed and was met with similar steel in the form of machine gun bullets, mortars and artillery. General Allen was faced with either obliterating the town of St. Cloud or going around it to Oran. He chose the latter, and sent units around St. Cloud to press on to Oran.

*Left to Right: Pvt. John Sckorupski, Sgt Fred Theiss, 2Lt. Berry near Arzew, Algeria early November 1943.*

Meanwhile, Allied forces tried to flank French forces in Oran on the 9th and met heavy resistance from the Vichy French. Allies captured the airport at La Senia and the 19th Engineers were sent there to set up their camp. Also on the 9th, the Germans turned west from Libya and invaded Tunisia to advance toward the Allies advancing to the German positions. (2.)

On the other side of Oran, led by Roosevelt, the landings continued with the same sort of chaos and speed. The French counterattacked on all fronts. Roosevelt was leading a column when he came across a man hiding behind a little hill. Roosevelt said, "Soldier, what in the hell are you doing here? Come on, follow me." The soldier followed with machine gun fire hailing around them.

There was little-to-no communication between the columns. None knew whether the other columns were making progress or were wiped out. Similarly, no one knew how the landings were going in Morocco and at Algiers. They, too, met resistance but advanced on schedule.

Finally, with the capture of La Senia and the circumvention of St. Cloud, the French saw that they were beaten. By dawn on November 10th, the 16th Infantry entered Oran and drove to the port.

Meanwhile, Berry's weapons platoon continued east along the railroad track all day on the 9th and all day on the 10th. The longer they went the hungrier they got and the more tired they became. The nights were cold and the troops were hungry, confused and lost in the desert.

On the 10th, commenting on British victories in North Africa, Winston Churchill made one of his famous speeches and said: "This is not the end. It is not even the beginning of the end. But it is, perhaps, the end of the beginning." Admiral Darlan, the commander of the Vichy French in Algeria, finally called on his French forces in North Africa to lay down their arms, while the Prime Minister of Vichy France, Laval, met with Hitler and Mussolini.

At 7:00 AM on the morning of November 11th, all French resistance in North Africa ended. At that very minute, an American column of trucks met Berry's platoon a long ways east of Arzew. An American Captain stuck his head out of a truck and said, "Are you guys Americans?" Berry responded, "Of course we are." The Captain said, "What are you doing way out here?"

The captain informed Berry's "rangers" that the invasion was complete and successful. They provided them with food, water and a ride back to Arzew and to rest of F Company.

*Cpl Jacob Kuntz and Cpl Bruce Weber of Berry's Weapons Platoon after arrival back to Arzew, November 11, 1943. Lt Berry shaved their heads and de-loused them.*

By then, F Company and 2d Battalion of the 19th had landed and had dispersed inland to a warehouse area near Arzew. F Company was bivouacked in an olive orchard wondering what had happened to Berry's weapons platoon. Upon arrival, LTC. Kellogg made all of the men that had been with Berry get their heads shaved and be treated for lice. On the 11th, Allied forces continued their advance easterly toward Tunis while more men, supplies, tanks and ammunition were unloaded in the harbors of Oran and Arzew. Fifth Army turned east and continued their advance toward Tunis.

*The headquarters compound of the French Foreign Legion at Sidi Bel Abbes.*

During the next few days, the company repaired bridges, cleared mine fields and repaired roads as the Allied forces continued to land and assemble in preparation for their drive toward Rommel's Afrika Corps.

Far to the west, Patton's task force was facing heavy fighting near Casablanca. Fighting lasted for three days and the American and British forces drove back Vichy French and French Moroccan units. At 2:00 AM on November 11th, the French surrendered to Patton.

By November 13th, the British had taken Tobruk and Eisenhower flew to Algiers to meet with Admiral Darlan to discuss surrender terms as well as terms to accept French forces into the Allied advance. 37,000 troops now occupied Oran and were

*Left to Right: Lt Joiner, Lt Whitis, Cpt Upton, Lt Buckner, of E Company. Note II Corp patch on Lt Buckner's left sleeve.*

*The "warehouse" district of Arzew housed the troops of the 19th Engineers.*

making the port ready to receive supplies.

In mid-November, Berry was ordered to take his platoon (now he commanded 3$^{rd}$ platoon) to repair an airport which had been bombed by the Allies. The airport was located about 40 miles south of Oran in a town called Sidi Bel Abbes, which housed the Headquarters of the French Foreign Legion in Algeria. At the time, the Vichy French were still fighting in some areas of Algeria and the Allies were still uncertain as to whether the French Foreign Legion was allied with the Germans or the Allies.

Berry loaded his platoon onto half-tracks and dump trucks and headed for Sidi Bel Abbes. They came upon the town and soon found the airport that had been bombed and destroyed by the Allies. Twenty-eight French airplanes were still parked on the apron and had been destroyed by Allied air power. Soon after they arrived, a French officer cautiously approached Berry and reported that his unit was prepared to work with the Americans. So, the French Foreign Legion men worked side by side with Berry's platoon to repair the runway. They found cement and made concrete to patch holes in the runway and taxiway and made other repairs to the airport complex.

The Algerian city of Sidi Bel Abbes was a colorful town made more so by the long history of the French Foreign Legion headquarters. The headquarters compound had a museum and was right on the edge of the Sahara Desert.

Allied forces that had landed in Algiers turned east as soon as they could and they drove as fast as they could toward the ports of Bizerte and Tunis. After

*Admiral Jean Darlan (left), commander of the Vichy French and Lt General Mark Clark at the signing of the armistice between the Vichy French and the Allies on November 22, 1942. (2.)*

53

the Vichy French switched sides, there was little-to-no opposition to the Allies which were spearheaded by the British. They went mostly overland through Northern Algeria and Tunisia and made nearly 500 miles in a week. Bizerte was only 45 miles away and Tunis only a short distance down the highway. But, unknown to the Allies, Rommel and the Afrika Korps had turned from the British to their east to the Americans and British to their west. They had crossed into Tunisia in order to protect Tunis and were ready to defend the Tunisian capital.

On November 17, 1942, while 3rd Platoon of F company was working at the airport at Sidi Bel Abbes, the British 78th Division met with German resistance for the first time during Operation Torch about 70 miles west of Tunis, Tunisia. The Germans fought ferociously and stopped the advance of the Allies. Finally, on November 20th the Allies retreated west. Admiral Darlan, however, repeated his orders to the men in French uniform in North Africa by saying, "I confirm to you my previous orders to fight at the side of the American and Allied forces for defense and liberation of our territories and integral restoration of French sovereignty."

*A French airplane similar to the one ridden by Lt Berry at Sidi Bel Abbes.*

Meanwhile, back at the airport at Sidi Bel Abbes, a French Lieutenant came up to Berry and told him that he wanted him to come with him and to fly with him. The French had put together one working airplane from the parts of the damaged fleet. As Berry's troops teased him about flying in the patched-up airplane, the two of them climbed into the airplane and the aviator started the engine.

They taxied to the end of the runway and suddenly crashed into a ditch at the end of the runway, to the loud laughter of both the French and Berry's men who were watching. Berry's men came and pulled the airplane out of the ditch with winches and the pilot worked again to fix the airplane.

The pilot was determined to get the airplane into the air and to show his flying skills to the Americans present.

So, the pilot insisted that they try to take off again. This time, they revved up the engines and raced down the runway and finally took off successfully. They flew around 100 miles around the coast and above Arzew and Oran, with Berry worried about crashing the whole time.

*Sgt Pittenger, 3rd Platoon Sergeant sporting his new haircut, near Arzew, November 1942.*

The 3rd Platoon stayed in Sidi Bel Abbes repairing the runway and airport buildings for about two weeks. At one time, Lieutenant Weed came down to visit Berry and 3rd platoon. Around November 25th, as the British First Army advanced to within 20 miles of Tunis, 3rd Platoon returned to their base camp in Relizane, Algeria about 55 miles east of Arzew.

Thanksgiving was uneventful for F Company. No turkey or dressing unless you were lucky enough to get a can of sliced turkey in your "C" ration box. The men were thankful that they were alive but all kept thinking of past Thanksgivings spent with family. German air power dominated the sky and reminded the men daily that they were at war. Luftwaffe attacks averaged about one per hour. Every soldier had an eye on the sky as he ate, cleaned his weapon or worked. German fighters seemed to lurk behind every cloud and they could come suddenly and without warning, spraying an area with machine gun fire or dropping bombs on groups of men.

F Company stayed in Relizane for several weeks as they continued to clear mines, build bridges and repair roads in the area east of Oran. Meanwhile, Allied forces were fighting desperate battles west of Tunis. The objective to capture Tunis within two weeks of the landings on November 8th had not been realized but the American and British armored columns, followed by infantry, pressed on, easterly toward Tunis.

*Tunisia Campaign operations 25 November to 10 December 1942. Courtesy, US Army.*

By November 9th, each of the three elements of the invasion turned east and raced toward Tunis. On November 27th, the Allied First Army was halted by the Germans in Tunisia between Terbourba and Djedeida.

German Panzer units were stopping the American lines with ferocious fire power. The Germans, too, were experienced fighters having fought the British in Libya and Egypt for the last three years. The Germans turned back the advancing Allies and the fight to Tunis was stalled while the Allies regrouped. On December 3rd, U.S. and French forces captured Faid Pass south of Tunis but the British were turned back at Tebourba by the German 10th Panzer after suffering heavy losses. The southern prong of First Army's drive on Tunis had been stopped but the Northern thrust toward Bizerte still looked promising.

At the same time, Eighth Army, under Montgomery in Libya, started an offensive towards Tebourba.

*Crusader III tanks in Tunisia, December 1942*

Patton's forces that had landed in Morocco headed east across the North African desert as well.

The men of F Company were still in Relizane, Algeria and slept in pup tents and ate "C" rations most meals. They continued to work to repair of roads and clear mines as well as unload supplies at Arzew. All wondered when they would be sent to the front.

On December 6th, sensing a weakness in the Allied line, the German 10th Panzer Division attacked along a one-mile front. Two waves of Stukas hammered the American 6th Armored Infantry Regiment which had dug in three miles southeast of Tebourba. Shortly, the American left flank was turned by German paratroopers. Then the German forces attacked the American right flank, crushing soldiers still in their foxholes.

The Germans kept coming and the Americans called for help and reinforcements. They didn't come soon enough and the American unit withdrew rapidly under fire, leaving scores of dead men, burned tanks and supplies. The defeat at Tebourba caused morale to slide and Allied soldiers didn't have the strut of victory or confidence of purpose that they once had. (2.)

Meanwhile the British were turned back and were retreating to within a few miles of Medjez and planned to retreat to a new line 15 miles west of the strategic city, much to the dismay of the French allies and Eisenhower. Instead, Ike ordered the British 1st Guards to move up to reinforce their British brethren at Medjez.

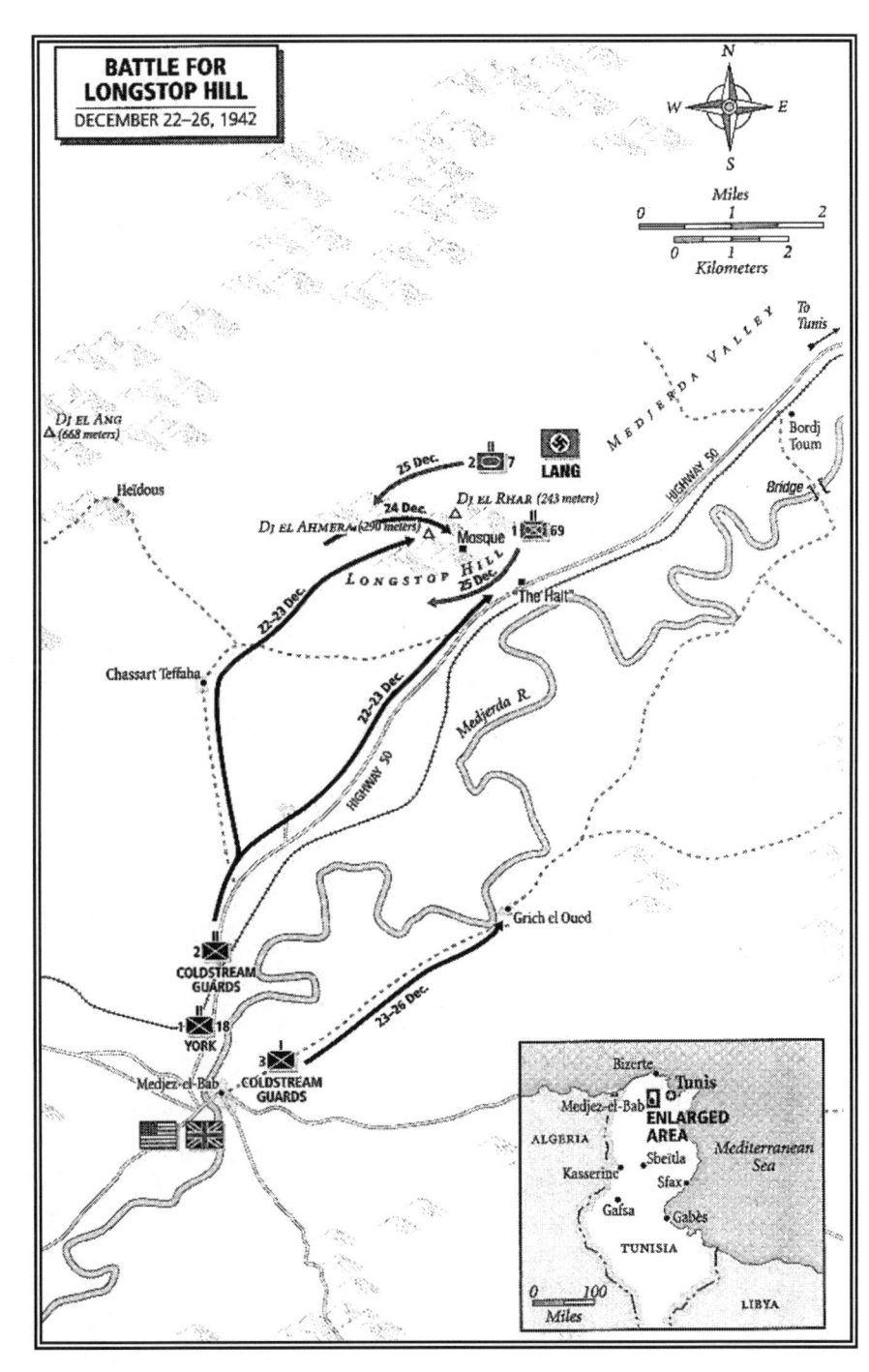

*The British and American advance in the Medjerda Valley, December 1942*

For eleven days in mid-December both armies licked their wounds, consolidated units and regrouped for action, along the Medjerda valley. Although 180,000 American troops were now in Northwest Africa, less than 12,000 of them were on the Tunisian front. The British had 20,000 men on the front while the French had 30,000 but Allied commanders discounted the fighting effectiveness of the French. Included with the 168,000 men who were not at the front in Tunisia were II Corps and the men of the 19th Engineer Regiment.

The Germans and Italians also were inventorying their positions. Axis troop strength in the Tunisian area had reached 56,000. They had about 160 tanks that was equivalent to the Allied number on line, however the Luftwaffe had air superiority in the theater. The 10th Panzer held the northern sector and the Italian Superga Division held the south.

It was decided by Eisenhower that the Allied offensive

should start on December 22$^{nd}$ with a three-pronged drive from Medjez northeast toward the German positions in the Medjaeda valley. The British Coldstream Guards would advance toward Grich el Oued on the right flank with another unit of the Guards supported by the American 18$^{th}$ Infantry advancing along Highway 50 to Longstop Hill which was occupied by the Germans.

The attack however was not planned well and Allied maps failed to show the terrain in the area. After the units advanced on the 22$^{nd}$, the Germans "came out of no where" the morning of the 23$^{rd}$ and surrounded units of the American 18$^{th}$ Infantry.

Artillery support was slow in helping and the Americans prepared to retreat from the heights but held on under heavy German fire. They were finally reinforced by elements of the Coldstream Guards.

Finally, on December 24$^{th}$, artillery came to the rescue and slowed the German advance. The Allies held the hill despite severe German counterattacks.

Meanwhile, back in Algiers, Admiral Darlan was assassinated by a French monarchist. Eisenhower was traveling to the front and was happy to hear that his units expected Longstop Hill to fall by the end of the day. However, on Christmas morning the Germans attacked on both flanks and caught the Allies off guard. The Allied right flank crumbled while German fire rained on Allied units in the rear area, suggesting that they were soon to be encircled.

*Christmas 1942, men of F Company get mail in Relizane, Algeria.*

Units on both flanks began to withdraw and as other units saw them retreat, a mass exodus occurred. By 9:00 AM, General Allfrey authorized abandonment of Longstop Hill. By noon, Longstop Hill belonged to the Germans while the Allied units retreated back to Medjez, leaving dead men and destroyed

*F Company on the streets of Relizane, Algeria, December 1942.*

equipment behind. (2.)

By the end of the year, the Allies had failed to reach any of their objectives. They had failed to take Tunis in two weeks. They had failed to take the fight into Libya and trap Rommel there. Although Montgomery's Eighth Army was advancing out of Egypt into Libya, Eisenhower's forces were not pinching Rommel from the west. Ike was depressed and knew that he had to address serious issues with his men. There were obvious tactical shortcomings in the U.S. Army as well as a lack of discipline among the men. It was believed by some that there was also a lack of valor – the desire to kill or be killed. That same day, Ike decided to stop the attack toward Tunis until the heavy rain ended.

The Americans had seen much. They had seen their friends and comrades killed. They had seen men on both sides crushed by tanks, or heads blown off or burned to beyond recognition by tank-mounted flame throwers. They had learned that combat was slower than expected and was more like a dance of forward, backward and sideways.

Heavy rains started on Christmas Day, 1942 and caused both sides to stop and to consolidate.

All during November the Allies continued to unload vehicles, men and supplies at the beach heads in northern Algeria. By late November, the 19th was equipped with half-tracks, 2½ ton trucks, dump trucks and jeeps. Berry was transported mostly in a jeep. The soldiers took advantage of nearby Relizane. A hair-cut, Turkish bath and a shave would cost about 3 cents. Soldiers traded with the local Algerians. Cigarettes could buy alot of local merchandise. Berry, for example, swapped a pack of American

*2Lt Berry, near Relizane, Algeria, December 1942, just after his area was strafed by German fighters.*

cigarettes for a clarinet.

As the fighting intensified on the Tunisian front, December 1942 meant more road repairs and clearing mine fields for the 19$^{th}$ Engineers. As Christmas approached, so did the rain.

December 31, 1942 found F Company still bivouacked near Relizane and 2Lt Berry was assigned as the duty officer for New Year's Eve. He was told by the Battalion commander, LTC. Kellogg, that he didn't want anyone firing weapons at midnight. Of course, it didn't matter what he did, at midnight someone started firing his weapon and once the first man started, dozens of others followed. Colonel Kellogg was mad but there wasn't much anyone could do.

Another "extra duty" common among lieutenants, was MP duty. Every night an officer of the 19$^{th}$ had to ride along with the MP's as they patrolled the various bars and taverns around Relizane, Arzew and Oran. Berry was the first officer to be assigned to this duty.

*Maj Gen Lloyd Fredendall, who later commanded the II Corps pins a purple heart on Bill Disher, a war correspondent who survived 25 wounds during Operation Reservist.*

That first night, 2Lt Berry was briefed by the commander of the MP's and was told that he had to write down every name of every soldier that had to be picked up because they were drunk or disorderly. Each one so caught would be court-martialed. Berry didn't care too much for this duty and didn't try too hard to find drunks.

During their time in the Relizane area, the 19$^{th}$ was assigned around 25 motorcycles to be used to perform reconnaissance. COL Moore made all of the 2d

*Lt. Davoust and Lt. Buckner, North Africa, December 1942.*

Lieutenants in the 19$^{th}$ learn how to ride the motorcycles. One evening, during a convoy to the front, Berry was riding his motorcycle at night and wrecked it, slicing his nose and ruining the motorcycle.

After that incident, Berry was relieved of having to ride them.

In early January, II Corps was ordered to the front, led by General Fredendall. Eisenhower wanted to resume the attack as soon as the weather cleared, especially in the south where the Axis line seemed to be the weakest. II Corps was finally going forward. The Corps convoyed southeast toward Tebessa and what had been nicknamed "Speedy Valley." In the front of the columns were the 19th Engineers clearing mines and building bridges so the columns could advance.

Just before leaving Relizane for Tunisia, Lt Weed was transferred out of F Company and into E Company where he joined Captain Murf Hawkins, Lt Jack Shirley, Lt Emil Buckner, and Lt Mike Davoust. F Company was still commanded by 1st Lieutenant Ed Pohlman, with platoon leaders Lt Berry, Lt Charlie Ellis, Lt Wilson Withers and Lt Mankoweicz.(1.)

Facing Fredendall's II Corps was Rommel's Panzer Army – Africa Korps. As the winter rains started to subside, the German army still held Longstop Hill in the north and were dug in on a line that ran due south through the heart of Tunisia. The important ports of Bizerte and Tunis were well within German hands while Eisenhower continued to bring troops to the Allied front.

On January 20, 1943, Eisenhower resumed the advance toward Tunis. At the same time, the German Army advanced from Tunis with the 5th Panzer going west toward Beja and Allfrey's 5th Corps. At the same time, Rommel's Panzers in the south advanced westerly along Highway 13 toward the Allies. Three days of fighting followed with neither side robust enough to win an advantage. Five battalions from General Allen's 1st Infantry Division joined Robinett in the north. By January 24th, the battlefield in Tunisia was stabilized with the German line approximately 8 miles further west than when the battles began. During this period, French losses were staggering, especially in the north where they were in support of the British.

*Sgt Floyd Terry on the road to the front, December 1942.*

In late January, II Corps reached the area of Tebessa, Algeria, an important crossroads near the stabilized front. General Fredendall established his headquarters in Tebessa and the 19th established headquarters in nearby Bou Chebka, about twenty miles to the east and that much closer to the front lines.

Eisenhower ordered Fredendall to defend the Allies' right while keeping his 1st Armored Division in reserve. Meanwhile, Rommel had re-armed and sent his 21st Panzer down Highway 13, attacking Faid Pass. Prompt decisive action may have saved Faid Pass which should have altered the grim task of the weeks to come. Instead Fredendall ordered a complicated series of maneuvers that only made matters worse and Faid Pass fell to the Germans.

*Two men of the 19th Engineers clearing mines in North Africa.*

French forces defending the pass pleaded for reinforcements as they took on the 21st Panzer and its might. As they waited and hoped for the much-needed reinforcements, the French fought ferociously against their recent allies who were determined more than ever to push the line to the west. But, due to Fredendall's incompetence, the French were not reinforced in time and the Germans, recaptured the pass on January 30, 1943.

*3rd Platoon, F Company, January 1943, somewhere in Tunisia. Lt Berry, front-center.*

The 19th Engineers spent most of January and early February repairing roads, clearing mines and rebuilding bridges in Tunisia as the Allies advanced. Much of the work had to be done at night as the skies

*US trucks from II Corps on fire after being strafed by German airplanes on the road to Kasserine, January 1943.*

often exploded with German fighters strafing units of the 19th. As the men of the 19th were dispersed along the front, they were bombed daily by German aircraft. Trucks that had been destroyed by the Luftwaffe littered the roads but the units continued to advance.

In early February, the first elements of Fredendall's II Corps reached Kasserine Pass in southwest Tunisia. Fredendall sent the 19th to the pass to clear the way for the advancing Allied columns in the Kasserine Pass valley. The 19th spent several days working in the pass as the Germans consolidated

*Lieutenant Berry during II Corps' drive east into Tunisia and toward Kasserine Pass, February 1943.*

northeast of the front.

On February 12$^{th}$, General Anderson, commander of ground forces in Tunisia, surveyed his positions. The British V Corps was in the North; the French were in the center, reinforced by Americans in reserve. In the south, Fredendall's II Corps was in place. The line seemed firm and ready for either an advance or defense of the line if the Germans attacked first.

On February 14$^{th}$, the German forces launched a powerful counter-offensive that took the Allies by surprise. The Germans attacked from the Faid Pass in Tunisia and broke through as the Allied forces withdrew to Sbeitla. Fierce fighting continued during the next few days with the Allies suffering heavy losses as the Germans advanced with heavy armor and Americans retreated in stunned confusion. Thus, the Battle of Kasserine Pass began. It was the first battle of World War II between the US Army and the German Army and the 19$^{th}$ Engineers would soon bear the brunt of the German juggernaut.

As the Allies withdrew, the 19$^{th}$ Engineer Regiment was left in the Kasserine Pass to continue its mission of clearing mines and repairing roads. Berry and the rest of F Company had been repairing bridges and building "shoe-flies" to allow II Corps vehicles to pass around streams and valleys. Suddenly, the German Army was bearing down on them and they were told to dig in and hold at all costs.

*Men of 3rd Platoon, F Company, 19th Engineers, digging a ditch for a railroad spur, January 1943.*

*Lt. Wilson V. Withers of F Company on the road to Kasserine, January 1943. He was killed in Sicily.*

*US II Corps trucks on fire after a German air attack, near Speedy Valley, January 1943.*

# The Battle of Kasserine Pass

The events that led to the Battle of Kasserine Pass began with Rommel's break-out at Faid Pass in late January. With Faid Pass in Axis hands, Rommel saw a way to split the Allies and to drive northwest from Faid through the Allies' supply area in Tebessa and on to the Algerian coast, thus encircling the northern Allied forces pressing in the north. He decided to attack through Sbeitla and then through Kasserine Pass to Tebessa. His route took him through the middle of the lines of Fredendall's II Corps which was spread too thin, from Gafsa in the South to Thala in the north.

On Sunday morning, February 14th, more than a hundred German tanks, including more than a dozen Tigers, left the western end of Faid Pass down Highway 13 past the sleepy burg of Faid and into the American lines at Sidi bou Zid. They swept through the American lines killing or capturing all in their path. Within minutes, American tanks in the path of the Germans were annihilated. American tank crews broke for the rear and artillery batteries pulled up stakes and fled. One by one, units were engaged with

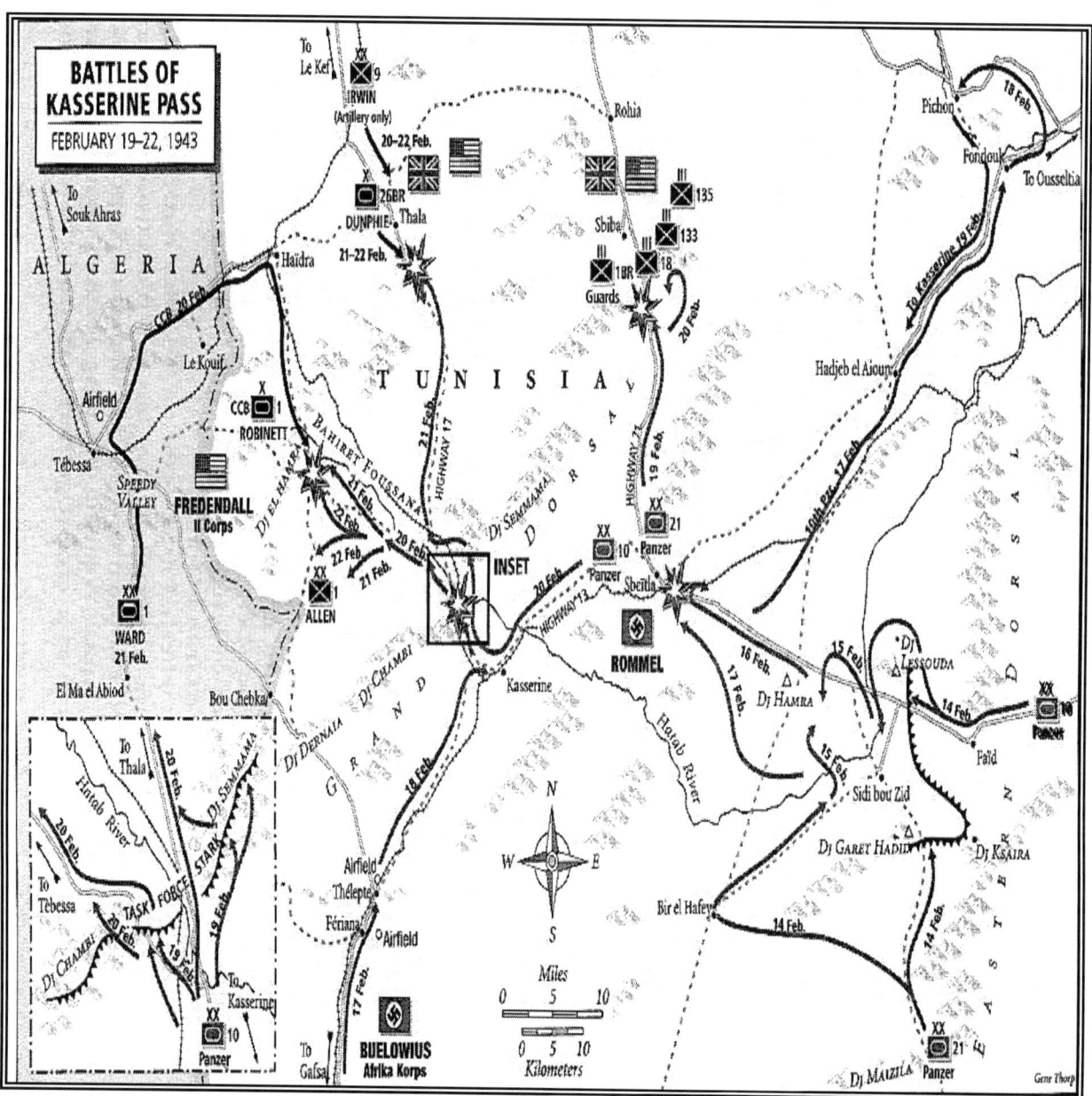

*Men of F Company carrying remains of downed American pilot of an A-20 bomber shot down right over their heads near Gafsa, Tunisia, April 1943.*

bullets, machine gun fire, mortars and artillery raining down.

Just as things seemed like they couldn't get any worse, Stukas arrived and attacked units south of Sidi bou Zid. Units continued to try to pull back amid the onslaught. By evening, the Germans had performed a double envelopment around Sidi bou Zid and American units were nowhere to be seen. They had retreated west or had been captured or killed. Some troops fought with uncommon valor while others didn't fight at all.

On February 15th and 16th, the Germans continued the attack attempting to drive all of the way West through II Corps to Tebessa, Algeria. The first defenders in the way were the Americans in the little town of Sbeitla. There were field hospitals in Sbeitla and many stragglers as well as refugees filled the town. Retreating soldiers from Sidi bou Zid fled to Sbeitla from the east believing that the Germans were bearing down on them. There was widespread panic as the Germans approached. As February 16th ended, the Germans were pouring down on Sbeitla.

That night General Ward phoned General Fredendall and told him that the Germans were coming hard and requested additional units. Fredendall moved units to Sbeitla to try to stop the Germans on the 17th. By then, his corps was in tatters and had been driven west over 50 miles with over 2,500 casualties and yet the Germans kept on coming. By nightfall, the Germans had taken Sbeitla with heavy Allied casualties.

Kasserine Pass is 25 miles west of Sbeitla and connects the Tunisian interior plateau to the Algerian highlands. The pass is the major pass through the Grand Dorsal mountains that run for 200 miles south from the Mediterranean Sea. Highway 13 runs right through the pass on trails that have served as invasion routes going both east and west for centuries. On February 17th, Fredendall had II Corps spread out throughout the southern theater licking its wounds from

Sbeitla and trying to cover more ground than it could with its forces. Suddenly, a force was desperately needed to defend Kasserine Pass from the German onslaught.

The 19th Engineer Regiment had arrived at the front in early January with the rest of II Corps. Since arriving at the front with the rest of II Corps, they had laid mines while the Corps was in a defensive posture, and removed mines laid by the Germans as II Corps advanced.

For several days, they had laid over 3,000 mines in front of the pass to slow any German initiative. When General Anderson arrived on the morning of February 17th, he saw that the II Corps was not well defended and that the Kasserine Pass was a likely approach by the Germans. He immediately ordered Fredendall to set up defensive positions in the pass. No other armored or infantry units were immediately

*Kasserine Pass from the German view from the east looking west. Dj. Chambi, the hill defended by F Company, is on the left and Dj. Semmama is on the German right. (10.)*

available so Fredendall ordered the 19th Engineer Regiment to set up defensive positions. The unit was not trained to fight as infantry and did not have the equipment or armor to defend against an infantry regiment, much less Panzers.

By 9:00 PM on February 17th, the 19th found itself as the lone defender of one of the most valuable topographic features of Tunisia. That night and the next day, the 19th dug in and prepared defenses while Rommel consolidated from his victory at Sidi bou Zid, refueled and prepared for his next attack – through the Kasserine Pass and the 19th Engineer Regiment.

Col. Moore, commander of the 19th, ordered the 19th to disperse on line perpendicular to the pass and to extend up into the hills on each side. They knew that they had to keep the Germans from flanking them by going around them through the hills. The men of the 19th only had small arms – M-14's and M-60 machine guns. But, they dug in as ordered and waited for the German tanks and armored personnel carriers to arrive, confident that they would drive them back.

The 19th Engineers were on line from left to right with companies A, B, C, D, E and F on line, so that A Company was on the far left of the line in the northern-most position and F Company was on the American right in the hills in the South. At that time, Berry commanded 3d platoon of F Company so only a few men were to his right, so he was nearly on the furthest point on the right flank of the Allied line. The 19th had placed over 3,000 mines in front of their lines to stop the German tanks. The right flank, where Berry had his platoon, covered a mountain on the south end of the pass called Dj. Chambi.

The Engineers laid additional mines in a triple belt in front of their positions. At that time, the 19th Engineer Regiment consisted of 55 officers, 1,350 enlisted men and about 150 vehicles, most of which were dump trucks and engineer equipment. Essentially none of the 19th had yet been under fire.

They built fox holes on line across the valley and waited. A senior officer came by and asked what their orders were and they explained that they were digging in to stop the Germans.

*The Germans destroyed the bridge in the background and the 19th Engineers constructed the bypass in the foreground, called a Tourna pull constructed on fill, near Kasserine, February 1943.*

Fredendall realized the vulnerability of the situation on the 18th of February and sent a battalion of the 1st Infantry Division along with a four-gun French artillery battery to help the 19th Engineers. This brought the total defenders to around 2,000 spread over a valley three miles wide. That same evening, Fredendall summoned Colonel Alexander Stark, commander of Allen's 26th Infantry Regiment. He phoned Stark and told him to get to Kasserine Pass right away and to defend the pass at all costs. It took him 12 hours to get to the pass, where he arrived at around dawn on February 19th, just as Rommel attacked.

At 5:00 AM on February 19th, the Africa Korps began its drive through the pass while the 21st Panzer drove north of the pass and 10th Panzer drove south of the pass. German and Italian forces began frontal assaults on the positions of the 19th Engineers in Kasserine Pass, which had been renamed Task Force Stark. At first the French battery was able to repulse the Germans as they advanced toward the pass but by 10:00 AM, German artillery started landing on the positions of the 19th. Soon after, German infantry advanced on the American left flank, hitting Company A of the 19th Engineers. By noon, German infantry was also attacking the hills on the American right, held by F Company. The American engineers had laid mines in front of their positions which stopped the armored advance for a while in front of F Company.

By evening on the 19th, the 19th Engineers and the support units had managed to repel the German advance. As the defenders were building their confidence, the theater commander, General Anderson, issued an edict to the units in the pass, "The army commander directs that there will be no withdrawal from the positions now held by First Army. No man will leave his post unless it is to counterattack."

However, men were at that very moment leaving their lines and withdrawing. Artillery shells and "screaming meemies", a multiple mortar shell, rained cats and dogs on the men in the line. One corporal in the 19th Engineers said, "I never knew that there could possibly be so many shells in the air at one time and so many explosions near you and still come out alive."

*American half-track near Kasserine Pass, February 1943. (12.)*

Officers managed to round up a few men fleeing to the rear but many kept going west out of the pass. Later that night, German elements overran the command post of the infantry battalion but the line somehow held throughout the night.

Although the fighting during February 19th had terrible results for the Americans, the next day was worse. On February 20th, Rommel sent an Italian Division toward the American right and the waiting soldiers of F Company. The Americans were crumbling in their positions but were still holding by mid-morning.

*March 1943, shortly after the Battle of Kasserine Pass, Lt Berry & Sgt Kiser stand next to a destroyed German half-track on the road to Gafsa. Notice the many bullet holes in the rear of the vehicle and that Berry is wearing a tie soon after Patton took command of II Corps.*

At that time, Berry's driver was Pvt Clarence O. Fulton who was from Canton, Ohio near Berry's hometown of Akron. Berry's 3rd Platoon was on line fighting the Italian advance. Fulton had taken the 50-caliber machine gun off of the mount on the jeep and had it emplaced in a fox hole on the line with Berry. During the ferocious fighting of the battle, Fulton fired the machine gun at the on-coming Italian and German infantry. One moment Berry heard the machine gun stop firing and turned to see that Fulton's head had been blown nearly off.

As the Italians attacked, Rommel ordered three more Panzer battalions into the attack with 10th Panzer still on the German right and Africa Korps on the German left, in front of F Company. Now the German army advanced with ferocity and the American positions collapsed by noon. At that time, COL Moore, the commander of the 19th, radioed Stark that the Germans were sweeping through the pass. Companies disintegrated into platoons and platoons into squads as soldiers raced to the rear any way they could make it. By 12:30 PM, Moore radioed, "Enemy overtaking our CP." When Moore himself got to Stark's position, he announced that the 19th Engineer Regiment no longer existed! By 3:00 Kasserine Pass was totally lost. Berry and his men raced down the west side of Dj. Chambi as the Germans pressed forward and took the heights.

Berry recalls that during the fighting at Kasserine Pass, Private John Sckorupski, a member of Berry's platoon, was hit in the helmet with a bullet. It knocked him down and knocked his helmet off. Sckorupski thought he was hit and dying. He lay on the ground and looked up at Berry and said, "Tell my girlfriend that I love her." Berry told him to get up, that he wasn't hurt. Sckorupski, indeed wasn't hurt but he wore the same helmet – with a bullet hole through it – for the rest of the war because he thought it was good luck.

The 19th Engineers was not obliterated but had 128 casualties, including Corporal Fulton. Altogether, Task Force Stark lost 500 killed, wounded and missing. The Africa Korps advanced for 5 miles west of

Kasserine Pass along Highway 13 toward Tebessa and saw no trace of Americans along the way.

The next day, Rommel decided to press the attack toward Tebessa while Fredendall lost all confidence in himself and his men. Alexander arrived from Egypt and took command of the 18th Army Group. What he saw was a shambles. American units were disorganized and generally had no idea of what their next move would be.

Men had seen death up close and had been overrun by the best of the German army. Some commanders were concerned that the Germans would press all the way through to Algeria.

Rommel decided to sweep south and try to surround the American II Corps and attack it from behind. He sent 21st Panzer in a northerly direction and Africa Korps south to envelope the American II Corps. However, both prongs were miraculously repulsed. American artillery were well positioned to pound the advancing German Panzers and the Germans lost

*Lt Berry in front of his jeep on March 8, 1943, a few days after the Battle of Kasserine Pass. F Company is rebuilding a bridge blown by the Germans while Lt Berry's driver, Pvt Alphonso Rocco, watches for German airplanes which often strafed them at work. Rocco was later killed in Italy when his jeep hit a mine. Note that Berry is looking sharp wearing his neck tie, as Gen Patton was appointed II Corps commander, two days earlier.*

*A bridge destroyed by the retreating German Army near Kasserine, March 1943.*

many infantry units to air and artillery attacks. The fighting continued on the 21$^{st}$ and the 22$^{nd}$ but Rommel was running out of supplies, ammunition, and men. Meanwhile, Eisenhower kept bringing up reinforcements to strengthen positions.

*An American artillery position in Tunisia pounding the advancing Germans in Kasserine Pass, February 1943.*

Finally, late on February 22nd, Rommel ordered a halt to the German drive and they pulled back easterly through Kasserine Pass that they had fought so hard to get. They gave up control of the pass because they seemed to know that they could not advance and, therefore, did not need it. They reassembled east of Kasserine, where they consolidated.

Meanwhile, the men of the 19th Engineers regrouped and reformed and fell in with the retreat of II Corps. The Regiment lost nearly all of their vehicles and many weapons and pieces of engineer equipment. Berry had reassembled his platoon and F Company was back in order licking its wounds. Communications between the companies were restored and the 19th was back to normal but without many of its men and devoid of most its equipment and vehicles.

On February 23rd, the Allies began their counter-attack and they re-took Kasserine Pass without a fight. As they came back through the pass, light snow fell on them. The landscape was cluttered with wrecked German and American airplanes, burned out vehicles, abandoned tanks and scattered shell cases. Nearby, Italian prisoners with black plumed helmets dug graves for bodies that were now ripe beyond recognition. As Rommel's units retreated east they left all nine bridges between Sbiba and Sbeitla demolished as well as thirteen others near Kasserine, leaving plenty of work for the remaining men of the 19th Engineers. As if the Engineers didn't have enough to do, the Germans laid 43,000 mines as they retreated. East of the pass, American vehicles were hitting mines all along the route as they pressed the advance.

*Men of 3rd Platoon, F Company, 19th Engineers, rebuilding a bridge destroyed by retreating Germans near Gafsa, March 8, 1943.*

The Germans, however, made advances in the north of Tunisia, driving back British and U.S. forces. The German advance was finally halted on the 27th near Beja, Tunisia.

II Corps experienced heavy losses during the fighting around Kasserine Pass, losing 6,500 men with total

*April 3, 3rd Platoon, F Company on a break while working on replacing a railroad bridge near Kasserine Pass after the battle. Parts of the demolished bridge can be seen in the background.*

*An American 37 mm cannon in position in Tunisia, 1943. (12.)*

Allied casualties at 10,000. Axis losses were around 2,000. American fighting men were badly humiliated at the Battle of Kasserine Pass. From Faid Pass to the final western line of the German advance west of the Kasserine Pass, the II Corps had been driven back 85 miles – further than would happen at the Battle of the Bulge two years later. American units lost confidence in themselves and in their leaders.

However, Rommel had finally been stopped and the Allies were retaking valuable ground while more reinforcements continued to arrive. At the same time, the Allies learned a valuable lesson about command structure and strategy in desert fighting.

*March 8, 1943. This is the same railroad bridge shown on page 74, built by 3rd Platoon, F Company with 23 men in 3 days at Kasserine Pass.*

For the next several weeks, II Corp regrouped. The 19th Engineers reassembled and were kept working night and day clearing mines that the Germans had left behind and rebuilding demolished bridges. Private Alphonso Rocco was in Berry's 3rd platoon and asked Berry if he could be his jeep driver after the death of Fulton. Rocco was from Ashtabula, Ohio, so Berry said yes to his in-state soldier. Rocco served as Berry's driver throughout the rest of the North African campaign as well as throughout Sicily and southern Italy. Rocco was killed in early 1945 in Empoli, Italy, a few miles west of Florence, when his jeep hit a mine.

While they re-grouped and reassembled, Eisenhower considered his command structure as well as his commanders. The first man to be relieved was his intelligence officer, General Eric Mockler-Ferryman. Eisenhower also relieved Colonel Stark. He was sent home on March 2 and later served with distinction in the Pacific. Next was General McQuillin. General Anderson was in the hot seat but managed to keep his job. Maj General Ward, commander of 1st Armored Division and detractor of General Fredendall, did not. Finally, Eisenhower conferred with several other general officers on his staff and relieved Fredendall as commander of II Corps. Fredendall slipped out of the area in a civilian car in the middle of the night on March 7th and returned home to a hero's welcome, received his third star and was placed in command of training an army in Tennessee.

Eisenhower chose George S. Patton to replace Fredendall as II Corps commander and Omar Bradley as his deputy. Patton arrived at Algiers with much fanfare on March 6th to meet Eisenhower and to take command of II Corps. On that same day, Rommel fought his last battle in North Africa while directing an offensive against British troops at Medenine. The Germans were routed, losing 50 tanks before retreating. Thereafter, Rommel was sent back to Germany to prepare German defenses of Italy and France for the coming Allied invasions.

Patton's first few days of command shocked and bewildered II Corps troops. Men were fined if they didn't wear ties properly and all boots and shoes were expected to be polished and clean.

Patton replaced lieutenants and captains right and left while demanding strict compliance with uniform

*A bridge being rebuilt by F Company next to a bridge destroyed by the retreating Germans, April 1943.*

regulations. He also forced officers to wear their metallic rank insignia which, most thought, were great for snipers to aim at. He also brought to the II Corps a sense of extreme hatred for the Germans. Although he was energetic and often jovial, he could also be abrasive and boorish while he insisted on his officers always thinking of attacking. Many nicknames were given to him but the one to stick the most was "Old Blood and Guts".

Soon after Patton took over II Corps, he visited a hospital in Feriana and tried to motivate many of the men who were lying wounded or hurt in their hospital beds. He asked one soldier how he got wounded and the soldier replied that he was shot while trying to surrender. "Serves him right – that's what he gets for trying to escape," exclaimed Patton to the hospital staff. This incident, of course, set the stage for his later, more famous faux paux in Sicily when he slapped a soldier in the hospital and called him a coward.

*Patton (left) with Rear Admiral Henry Kent Hewitt aboard USS Augusta, off the coast of North Africa, November 1942*

*German prisoners captured during the Allies advance east from Kasserine Pass. Most look pretty happy - the war is over for them and they are headed for a prisoner of war camp in the US.*

*Lt Berry & Lt Emil Buckner a few days after the Battle of Kasserine Pass, next to a destroyed bridge abutment, near Tebessa, March 4, 1943.*

*Elements of the 19th Engineer Regiment laying mines in Kasserine Pass, February 1943. The mines were laid to slow a possible advance by the Germans westerly through the pass. The mines did, indeed, slow the German advance when Rommel initiated an all-out attack through the pass. Anti-personnel mines were laid mixed in with anti-tank mines. The men of the 19th Engineers defended the pass against the German attack and covered the mine fields with fire from artillery and mortars, as well as small arms.*

*A bridge rebuilt by Sgt Pittenger's squad in F Company after destruction by retreating Germans. The squad finished in only 4 days, south of Sbeitla, Tunisia, March 1943.*

*Lt Berry and a member of his platoon in March 1943 as the Allies advanced east from Kasserine Pass. They're joking around about something related to their crotch.*

*Lieutenant Charlie Ellis looking at a dead German tanker inside his burned-out tank. The smell was awful, near Ksar Mesowr, Tunisia April 1943.*

*Lt Berry next to a dead Austrian soldier near Hill 609 at Sidi Nsir, Tunisia, May 1943. The body of the dead soldier was booby trapped. It was full of snails, maggots and stench. A few minutes after the picture was taken a medic went to move the body and the booby traps exploded and killed the medic.*

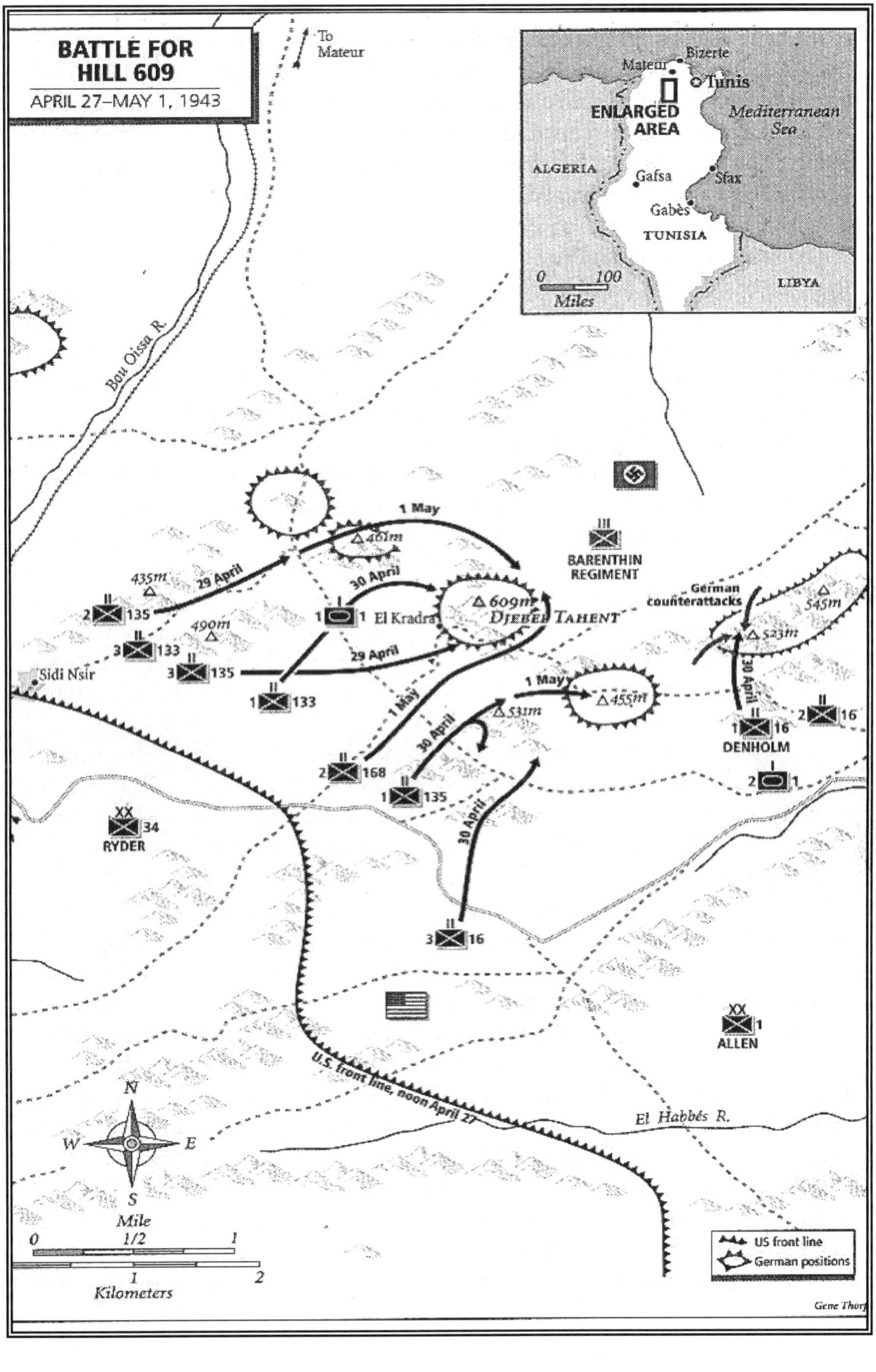
BATTLE FOR HILL 609
APRIL 27–MAY 1, 1943
To Mateur
Bizerte
Mateur
Tunis
ENLARGED AREA
Mediterranean Sea
ALGERIA
Gafsa
Sfax
Gabès
TUNISIA
LIBYA
0 100 Miles
Bou Oissa R.
1 May
461m
BARENTHIN REGIMENT
435m
29 April
30 April
German counterattacks
545m
135
609m
El Kradra
Djebel Tahent
133
490m
523m
Sidi Nsir
29 April
1 May
455m
531m
30 April
16
DENHOLM
168
1 May
30 April
34
RYDER
30 April
ALLEN
U.S. front line, noon April 27
El Habbés R.
N
W
E
S
Mile
0 1/2 1
1 2
Kilometers
US front line
German positions
Gene Thorp

For the next two weeks, the Axis and Allied forces pierced each other's lines from north to south with no major encounters.

On March 16th, Montgomery launched an offensive with the British Eighth Army into southern Tunisia from Libya with the objective of taking the Tunisian port city of Mareth and then driving north along the Mediterranean Sea to eventually capture Gabes and Sfax and, thereby, drive the Germans solely into northern Tunisia around Tunis and Bizerte. At that point, the Allies would have the British Eighth Army, the British First Army and the American II Corps on line and prepared for the final drive to Tunis

*A destroyed German jeep near Kasserine, March 1943.*

Patton was ordered to support Montgomery's left flank and to "avoid any major conflicts" as the British did not want Patton gumming up the works. On March 16th, Patton received his third star from Eisenhower and, thusly, was promoted to the rank of Lieutenant General. That evening, he called together his staff officers and despite his orders to the contrary, told them, "Gentlemen, tomorrow we attack. If we are not victorious, let no one come back alive."

On March 17th, despite Eisenhower's directive, Patton's II Corps went on the offensive in Tunisia with the mission to take Gafsa. The area in front of the town had been heavily mined so, as usual, the 19th Engineers led the way so that Patton's armor could advance. Gafsa was taken quickly, but, mostly because the defenders retreated quickly as they were largely outnumbered.

On March 21st, the II Corps made strong gains as they continued their push toward Tunis. They executed an encirclement around German forces capturing over 700 Axis soldiers near Djebel el Ank.

*Cpl Jackson, Staff Sgt Terry and Staff Sgt Palmquist at Ksar Mesour, Tunisia, April 1943 next to a Mark VI Tiger tank destroyed by artillery and dive bombing by Allied planes. Sergeant Palmquist was killed later in Italy.*

On March 22nd, II Corps turned northeast, with the 19th in the lead, toward Tunis as the three-pronged Allied advance continued. The 19th was working day and night clearing mines in front of the Corps' advance and rebuilding bridges that the Germans were knocking down as they retreated.

Heavy rains slowed their progress but the II Corps continued its push toward Tunis. As they advanced one day in late March 1943, Berry and Ellis' platoons were together clearing a minefield. There was a convoy of trucks and tanks waiting for the 19th to clear the mine field in order to pass through the area. As they were in the process of clearing the mines, they came across a particular unexploded bomb that had landed in the middle of the road near the intersection of the road and a railroad track. "It was the biggest bomb we'd ever seen", Berry reported later. It was much bigger than a person; we thought it weighed about a ton. Berry and Lt Ellis began to look at the bomb and were in the process of figuring out whether to defuse the bomb or to blow it in place. They radioed to the company commander, Cpt Pohlman, and asked whether to blow the bomb or defuse it.

At that moment, General Patton, who had been following the tank and truck convoy, drove up to the site to see what was holding up the column. He got out of his jeep with all the fanfare that he was used to, walked over to Lieutenants Ellis and Berry, and asked them what was holding up the column. Berry explained that there was a large, undetonated bomb in the middle of the road and that they were trying to decide whether to blow it in place or to defuse it.

They asked Patton, "should we go ahead and blow-up the bomb?" Berry explained that if they blew it, they would have to fill in the hole caused by the explosion and that would take a few minutes. General Patton then asked Lt. Ellis, "What gauge is that bomb?" Ellis remarked that he didn't know. Patton, then pulled out his pistol and told Ellis, "The barrel of his pistol is .45 caliber, use it to figure out the caliber of the bomb."

Lieutenant Ellis calculated the size of the bomb and Patton told them to go ahead and blow it. Berry's platoon packed dynamite around the bomb and they then fired a bazooka (anti-tank weapon) at the bomb so that it exploded. It took the two platoons about an hour to fill in the hole so that the tank column could pass. This was Lt Berry's first, but not last, encounter with General Patton. Somehow, he and Lt Ellis had managed to get through the incident without being demoted or court martialed!

From March 23rd to April 3rd the II Corps fought the Battle of El Guettar, east of Gafsa. There was extremely heavy fighting on both sides as the Americans tried to envelope the German 10th and 21st Panzer Divisions. American units were repulsed time after time, much to the dismay of Patton. The 1st Infantry Division – the Big Red One, the 47th and the 9th Infantry Divisions made frontal assaults at German positions near El Guettar time and time again. But, each time, hundreds of men were killed by German tanks and artillery as well as German infantry who were dug in and who fought ferociously.

Artillery poured down onto both sides and fighting was brutal as the Americans were determined to drive back the Germans and the Germans, in kind, were determined to hold. Tank battles set tanks and their crews ablaze and dead soldiers riddled the desert floor. The battle had meant to lure panzers away from Montgomery's drive north and it had worked.

*A bridge destroyed by the retreating Germans, east of Kasserine Pass, March 1943.*

The Battle of El Guettar is not a well-known battle but was a terrible battle with thousands of casualties on both sides. Losses were extremely heavy and when the Germans finally withdrew, it marked the beginning of the end of German occupation of Tunisia and North Africa.

The Battle of El Guettar is also the battle depicted in the movie, "Patton" in which Patton's aide is killed and his deputy commander, General Omar Bradley is nearly killed when his jeep is hit with artillery.

*Lt Berry with Tunisian nomads at the base of a bridge, April 1943.*

Patton's actual aide, Captain Richard Jenson, died on April 1st near El Guettar, as Bradley was nearly killed on the same day. In the movie as well as in the actual incident, General Patton was present at Captain Jenson's funeral and praised his courage.

Two days later, another incident occurred that was also depicted as a scene in the famous movie. On April 1st, during the Battle of El Guettar, Air Marshal Tedder and Lieutenant General Carl Spaatz, the two most senior air commanders in North Africa, went to Gafsa to discuss the situation with Patton and try to explain to him that the Allies, indeed, had air superiority and that the II Corps was covered.

In the middle of the meeting, as Patton was pounding his fist on the conference table, three German fighters roared over Gafsa firing machine guns and strafing the streets all around the building in which the meeting was taking place. The planes made a second run and dropped bombs around the plaza, one of which went almost right through the conference room. As bullets flew and bombs exploded, Patton ran outside and fired his pistols at the fighters.

When Patton returned, Air Marshal Tedder asked how Patton had arranged that show at that time. Patton responded, "I'll be damned if I know, but if I could find the sonsabitches who flew those planes, I'd mail each one of them a medal".

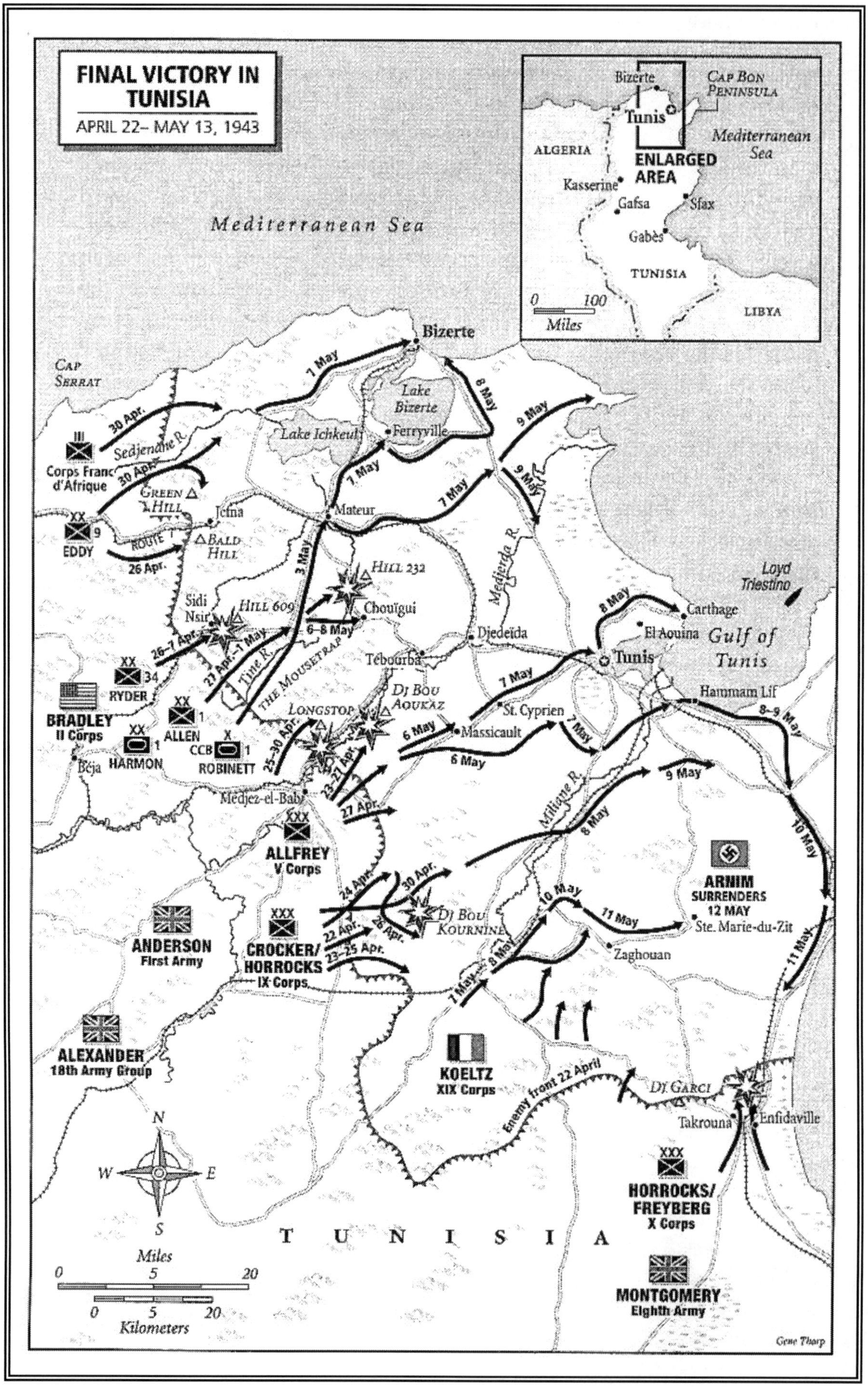

FINAL VICTORY IN TUNISIA
APRIL 22– MAY 13, 1943
Bizerte
Cap Bon Peninsula
Tunis
Mediterranean Sea
ALGERIA
ENLARGED AREA
Kasserine
Gafsa
Sfax
Gabès
TUNISIA
LIBYA
0 100
Miles
Mediterranean Sea
Bizerte
Cap Serrat
Lake Bizerte
Lake Ichkeul
Ferryville
Sedjenane R.
Corps Franc d'Afrique
Green Hill
Jefna
Route 7
Bald Hill
EDDY
Mateur
Hill 232
Chouïgui
Sidi Nsir
Hill 609
Medjerda R.
Djedeïda
Tebourba
Tine R.
The Mousetrap
RYDER
BRADLEY
II Corps
ALLEN
HARMON
CCB
ROBINETT
Béja
Longstop
Dj Bou Aoukaz
Massicault
St. Cyprien
Tunis
Carthage
El Aouina
Gulf of Tunis
Loyd Triestino
Hammam Lif
Medjez-el-Bab
ALLFREY
V Corps
Milliane R.
ARNIM
SURRENDERS
12 MAY
Ste. Marie-du-Zit
Dj Bou Kournine
Zaghouan
ANDERSON
First Army
CROCKER/
HORROCKS
IX Corps
ALEXANDER
18th Army Group
KOELTZ
XIX Corps
Enemy front 22 April
Dj Garci
Takrouna
Enfidaville
HORROCKS/
FREYBERG
X Corps
MONTGOMERY
Eighth Army
T U N I S I A
N
W
E
S
Miles
0 5 20
0 5 20
Kilometers
Gene Thorp

After the battle, Patton relieved Major General Ward, commander of the 1st Armored Division on April 5th. On April 6th, the Germans finally withdrew north toward Tunis. They were increasingly outnumbered as Allied reinforcements and re-supply shipments supported their fight while the Germans were not resupplied. Of the Battle of El Guettar, the Big Red One's operations officer said it was "the most severe battle of the three years of warfare", which included the division's fighting in Sicily, Normandy and Aachen.

*The 19th Engineers convoying near Sidi Bou Zid, Tunisia, just after being strafed by German fighters, advancing toward Tunis, April 1943.*

The Battle of El Guettar is also where, spurred on by the ruthlessness of Patton, many American units learned to really hate the Germans and to really want to slaughter them. Many of the units of II Corps were solidified into a fighting force after the horrible fighting and many frontal assaults over the more than two weeks of fighting.

The Allies pressed on toward Bizerte. In mid-April, F Company was clearing mines and repairing roads along the main road to Bizerte. In the middle of the day, a jeep came by distributing US Army newspapers to the troops. The paper was called "Stars and Stripes". Lt Berry was anxious to take a break and to get out of the sun so he took a paper and sat in the back of a truck in the shade to read the latest about the war. About that time, someone in 3rd platoon yelled out, "Patton's coming!". In those days, Gen Patton was relieving officers daily for various infractions. Most officers, especially lieutenants, were scared to death of "Old Blood and Guts".

Lt Berry jumped up and looked down the road and saw General Patton's group coming down the road with flags flying. Of course, all of the troops immediately jumped to attention while General Patton pulled off of the road and asked, "What are you troops doing?" Lt. Berry jumped to attention and said that they were repairing chuck holes. Patton said, "When is the last time that you have had fresh meat?" One of the troops said, "Sir, we have only had 'C' Rations since we landed in November – we haven't had any fresh meat since then!" Patton turned to one of his staff officers and said, "See to it that these men get a hot meal out here." And, off they went.

About two days later a truck convoy came loaded with food. Army Air Corps troops showed up with all manner of food. They all seemed scared to be so close to the front. They unloaded frozen turkeys, ham and beef for the 19th mess to prepare for the men.

*Men of the 19th Engineers building a timber trestle bridge in northern Tunisia, May 1943, during the final drive to Tunis.*

The II Corps kept up the forward pressure while the Germans continued their stubborn defense. Next, the Battle of Fondouk Pass pushed the Germans further north to near the outskirts of Tunis while they pulverized the oncoming Allied infantry.

*A bridge being rebuilt, by Sgt Pittenger's squad in F Company after destruction by retreating Germans. The squad finished in only 4 days, south of Sbeitla, Tunisia, March 1943.*

On April 20th, Patton was replaced as commander of II Corps in order for him to begin preparation for the invasion of Sicily, which Eisenhower wanted him to lead. Patton's deputy, General Omar Bradley was given command of the Corps. On that same day, the final push to Tunis and Bizerte began.

*A German tanker crushed under his own tank, Tunisia, April 1943.*

General Alexander, commander of the 18th Army Group and overall commander of ground forces in Tunisia, had British and French forces in the far north drive east toward Bizerte; II Corps, now commanded by Bradley, was south of the French and British units, and drove northeast, also toward Bizerte; Allfrey's V Corps was aligned south of II Corps and drove toward Tunis with Montgomery's Eighth Army driving north toward Tunis.

On April 27, 1943, II Corps and the 19th Engineers clashed with German forces at Hill 609. The 19th continued the mission to clear mines near and on the hill. Fighting continued with the Allies pressing forward and fighting for every inch of ground. German and Italian forces were being pinched from all sides and were fighting with their backs against the wall

*Lt. Berry and Lt. Wilson Withers at Beja, Tunisia, April 7, 1943. Lt. Withers was later killed in Sicily.*

*Corporal Lambert repairing a bridge abutment, Tunisia, April 1943.*

*Cpt Ted Hoster of Annapolis, Maryland, North Africa, 1943.*

*Lt Bob Weed shortly after the Battle of Kasserine Pass, February 1943.*

Finally, on May 12, Germany's commander, General Arnim, surrendered the Axis forces and the war in North Afric was over. Lt Berry spent time in Tunis and then in Bizerte. In Tunis, F Company came across an American civilian couple who had been stranded in Tunis.

As June 1943 approached, Tunisia was solidly in Allied hands and Eisenhower was preparing for the pending invasion of Sicily. Three lieutenants from the 19th were assigned to go onto the ships that had been assigned to take the 19th to Sicily during the next invasion. The lieutenants were to supervise getting them ready to load troops and equipment.

So, the three lieutenants, Berry, Weed and Buckner, were ordered to the port at Oran, Algeria where they went and waited for further orders and to prepare the ships to house troops for the invasion of Sicily. Finally, after three days, Lt Weed was assigned to a nice Dutch ship and was assigned a state room. The next day, Lt Buckner was assigned to a nice British ship. Finally, Lt. Berry was assigned a "liberty" ship, the HMS Empress Snipe, which was in bad repair. After a few days of work, the three ships sailed east to Bizerte where the 19th would load and embark to Sicily.

*After the German surrender of Tunisia, Lts Weed, Buckner and Berry were sent to Oran to prepare ships to haul F company from Tunisia to Sicily for the coming invasion. This photo is taken of Berry's ship, the HMS Empress Snipe. It had been an American "Liberty" ship as it was given to the British prior to the war. It had been used by the British to haul men and supplies for over two years and had been in the Mediterranean theater for over 15 months. While the rest of F company was back at Tunis, this ship, along with those prepared by Buckner and Weed, had been prepared for the invasion of Sicily by Berry and the crew and were sailing from Oran to Tunis as this photo was taken. This ship was full of gasoline in the front two holds and carried bombs in the rear holds. This is a shot of the crew of the HMS Empress Snipe with Lt Jerry Berry on the far right in his uniform.*

Work continued on the ships and the lieutenants were pretty unhappy that they were stuck on the ships and could not go to shore. After a few more days, a radioman on board the HMS Empress Snipe, Berry's ship, came up to him and asked if he knew a Lt. Weed. After the affirmative response, the radioman said that he had just received a signal that Lt. Weed was rowing toward Lt. Berry's ship.

Sure enough, there was Weed in a small rubber boat, paddling toward Berry's ship. Berry yelled out: "Weed, what are you doing?" Weed said, "I'm going after the mail!" Weed paddled on to shore, got the mail for the men on the three ships, and returned.

*Lt Weed, front-center, and 2d Platoon, F Company, near Bizerte, Tunisia, June 1943.*

*The British Eighth Army having a Victory Parade, Tunis, May 1943.*

*F Company troops on R&R in Oran, June, 1943.*

*Lt. Berry, near Bizerte, July 1943. His II Corps shows proudly on his left sleeve.*

*Left to Right : Pvt Collins (later wounded ); Pvt Wehrle; John Mata; and, Lt Berry, on R&R in Oran, Algeria, June 1943.*

*Lt. Berry and a lieutenant friend on R&R in Tunis, after the surrender of German forces in Tunisia, June 1943.*

*Cpt Moulton, Lt Joiner and Lt Weed, Tunisia, early July 1943.*

*Lt Berry on R&R at the beach near Oran as he waits for his ship to be readied, June 1943. He, Weed and Buckner stayed at a hotel next door to the women's R&R hotel in Oran and enjoyed the beaches there while waiting for their Liberty ships to be made ready for the invasion of Sicily.*

*Lt Berry around late June 1943 after the North African campaign is over but before the invasion of Sicily.*

*Lt Berry in North Africa.*

*The HMS Tintern Abbey in front and the HMS Empress Snipe, behind, in Oran Harbor, 1943, being outfitted to carry the men and supplies of the 19th Engineer Regiment to the beaches of Sicily.*

*While Berry, Buckner and Weed were in Oran and their Liberty ships were being outfitted, they were able to take a break on the beaches of Oran. This building served as the women's R&R Hotel in Oran and was next door to the hotel that the F company officers used. There are two unidentified soldiers in a jeep in the foreground and two others climbing the stairs on the right.*

*A small USO show near Tunis, May 1943.*

# Invasion of Sicily

As the Allies were winning in Tunisia, plans were being made for the invasion of Italy through Sicily. One plan, code-named Operation Trojan Horse, was developed by MI-6, Great Britain's Intelligence branch. The plan was to try to conceal the Allies' intentions to invade Sicily by planting false information so the Germans would think the invasion would be elsewhere from Greece to southern France. On April 30, 1943, the body of a Royal Marine officer whose papers identified him as a Captain William Martin, floated ashore at Huelva, Spain. He had apparently died in a plane crash and appeared to be an important courier, for a dispatch case was still attached to his arm. In the case was a top-secret document that indicated conclusively that the Allies were going to invade either Greece or Sardinia, not Sicily. Such were the preparations that the Allies tried all sorts of trickery. Although everyone on both sides knew that Sicily would be the target, Operation Trojan Horse made the German high command stop and consider this new possibility.

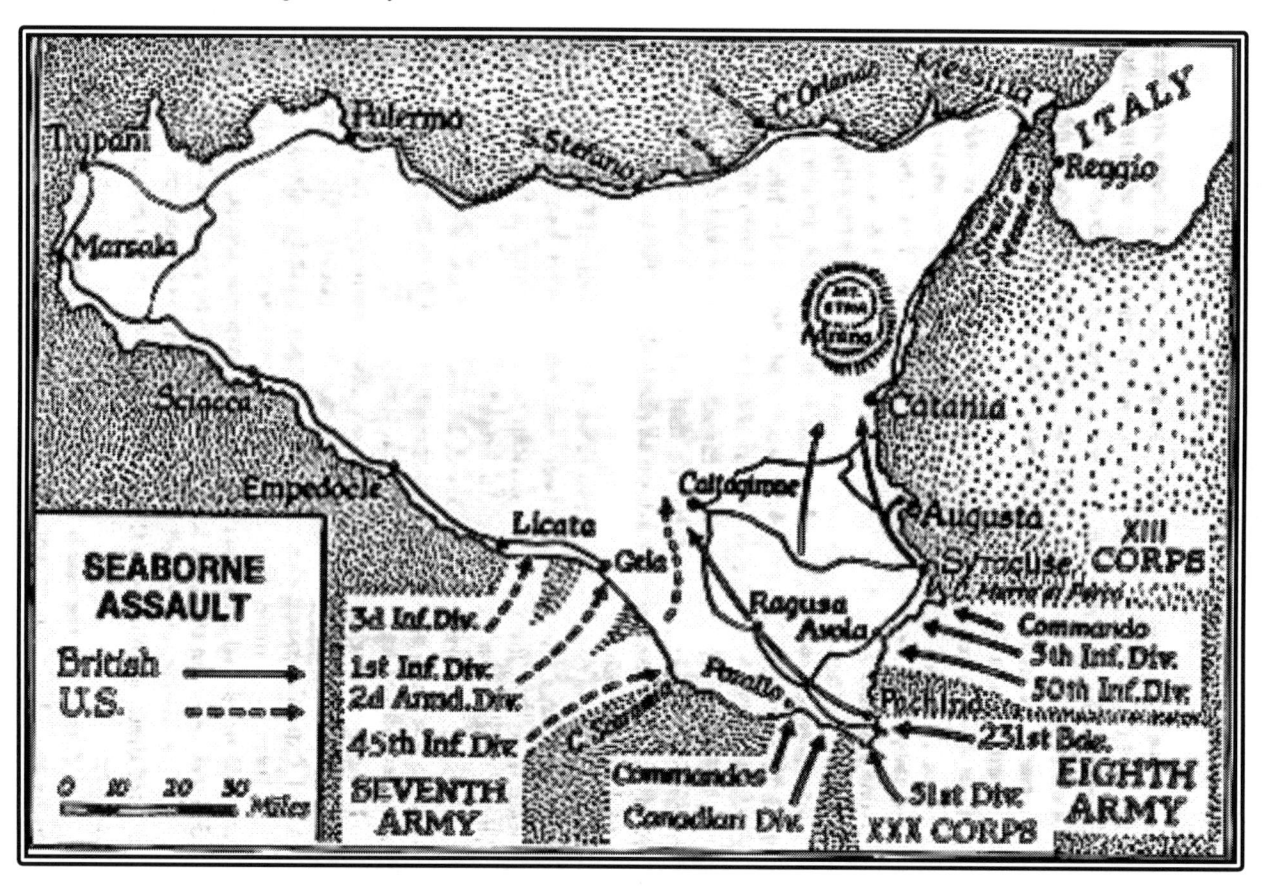

Hitler, especially, wanted to believe that the Allies would not invade Sicily and some troops were shifted to both Greece and Sardinia just in case. The poor man in the uniform was actually a civilian that had died of pneumonia and had been packed in dry ice and prepared for his involuntary duty. (11.)

As the Allies were preparing for their invasion of Sicily, so too were the Axis powers preparing to meet the invading forces. Field Marshall Herman Kesselring was commander of the theater with the Italian General Alfredo Guzzoni in command of the Axis forces in Sicily. General Frido von Senger was at Guzzoni's side as commander of the German forces on the island and was also there to make sure the

Italians fought when the time came. General Paul Conrath commanded the elite Hermann Goering Division which was carefully positioned in Sicily to drive any invaders back out to sea.

On June 10, 1943, after the fall of Tunisia, General Eisenhower called a press conference in Algiers where he astounded the group by announcing that the Allies would invade Sicily in early July. He further announced that the British Eighth Army under General Montgomery would attack the eastern beaches north of Syracuse and that the Seventh Army commanded by General Patton would attack the southern beaches. He also announced that the Allies would use airborne troops on a much larger scale than had previously been used. Eisenhower knew that the reporters could not print the story because of its classification and that if the Germans heard of the announcement through a spy, they would discount it as a ruse.

As the day of the invasion approached, Allied plans were finalized. The plan, called Operation Husky, called for parachute and glider elements of the U.S. 505th Regimental Combat Team, part of the 82nd Airborne Division, to land north of Gela and to secure routes to the beaches there until the American 7th Army could land and relieve the paratroopers. Meanwhile, the British 1st Air Landing Brigade were to land gliders full of paratroopers near Syracuse, on the east coast of Sicily. The British 1st were called the Red Devil Brigade.

Soon after the American and British paratroopers landed early on July 9th, the US Seventh Army under Patton would land near Gela and the British Eighth Army under Montgomery would land near Syracuse. In the initial assault, there would be 160,000 men, nearly 3,000 ships and landing craft, 14,000 vehicles, 600 tanks and 1,800 guns taken ashore. General Eisenhower would position his headquarters nearby on the island of Malta. Patton and Montgomery reported to General Harold Alexander, commander of the

*General George Patton coming ashore at Gela, Sicily, 1943.(11.)*

Fifteenth Army.

Meanwhile, General Omar Bradley was still the commander of the US II Corps, which was assigned to Seventh Army and which would lead the American invasion. II Corps include the two battalions of the 19th Engineer Regiment. Maj General Lucien Truscott commander of the U.S. 3rd Infantry Division,

*German planes bomb the American convoy off of Gela, Sicily, July 10, 1943. (8.)*

bellowed over a loud speaker to his troops, "You are going to meet the Boche soon. Carve your name in his goddamned face." Also included in the II Corps were the 1st Infantry Division commanded by Terry Allen and the 45th Infantry Division, who would simultaneously storm the beaches at H hour.

Fresh from their conquest of Morocco, Algeria and Tunisia, the Allied forces under Eisenhower were confidently preparing for the massive invasion of Sicily, the first invasion of the shores of an Axis country. The 18th Army Group had been reinforced, re-equipped, and rejuvenated while the logisticians made final plans for the great invasion. The Axis powers were, too, ready. All of the men knew that many would be killed.

The German forces expected to drive the Allies back out to sea like they had done at Dunkirk in 1940. The Allied forces believed they would, themselves, be victorious. The Axis powers included divisions of Italians defending their homeland. The Allied forces included thousands of Italian-Americans determined to liberate Italy from the domination of Mussolini's Fascist government. The stage was set and the entire world watched.

*American parachute troops make last-minute adjustments to their packs and parachutes before boarding the C-47 transport which will carry them to drop zones in Sicily, July 9, 1943. They wear American flags sewn on their right arm. (8.)*

On July 5, 1943, the massive invasion of Sicily got under way. American and British troops and vehicles were loaded onto ships in Tunisia as well as elsewhere. Lt Berry's ship, HMS Empress Snipe, which he had helped to prepare, was loaded with troops of the 19th Engineers at Bizerte, Tunisia, while other elements of Patton's Seventh Army departed from the ports of Algiers and Oran. The British Eighth Army departed from the ports of Benghazi, Tripoli, Port Said, Alexandria, Beirut and Haifa. In a few days, the two massive convoys converged on southern Sicily.

Around midnight on July 6th, an urgent message was handed to General Guzzoni at his sixth Army headquarters in the ancient walled town of Enna in central Sicily. The commander responsible for defending the island had put in his customary 17-hour day, when he started reading: "You are to defend Sicily at all costs." It was signed Benito Mussolini. (11.)

The evening of July 9th, planes full of British and American paratroopers and glidermen took off in a full moon from locations in North Africa toward their destiny on Sicily.

*Unloading vehicles, men, weapons and supplies of the 19th Engineer Regiment at Gela harbor, Sicily, July 1943.*

**Lt Weed devised a crane extension to raise timber and steel members to help bridge wide gaps in Sicily. "Weed's Derrick" is seen at work here at a bridge site in Sicily, August 1943.**

Just after midnight on July 10th, American paratroopers landed as planned north of Gela and secured the high ground to protect the port city. German forces witnessed the airborne assault and shot down a number of gliders and aircraft carrying paratroopers.

As the 82d Airborne troops were searching for their assigned positions in the darkness, Italian and German troops were being sent to defend the island. General Guzzoni was sent reports from commanders in the field and was assigning assault units to drive the Americans back to the sea. However, he had a wide array of information which pointed to American units in many conflicting places.

*British troops land on Sicily at dawn on July 10, 1943 near Syracuse. A fleet of 3,000 ships converged on designated points and troops, guns, tanks, and supplies were rushed ashore under incessant bombardment by enemy artillery. (8.)*

The Italian and German forces had spotted the Allied sea convoy and Guzzoni knew that the invasion by sea was about to happen.

Meanwhile at 1:00 AM American troops of the II Corps were loading into landing craft in high seas. Many of the men became violently ill from sea-sickness from the rolling boats. American warships started pounding the beaches at Gela with heavy guns at 1:30. Soon, landing craft were leaving their ships for the nine-mile launch to the beaches at Gela.

At 2:45 AM leading elements of the 1st Infantry Division and the 45th Infantry Division stormed ashore at Gela under the watchful eye of General Bradley who was on the USS Ancon positioned in the Gulf of Gela with hundreds of other craft, including those which held the 19th Engineer Regiment. Resistance was fairly light and the only place where the Germans challenged the landings were at Gela against the Big Red One – the 1st Infantry Division. (11.)

The 19th Engineers landed in southern Sicily at Gela under fire from German positions nearby. The infantry and engineers advanced, driving back the German forces and secured the airport nearby. Assigned to Bradley's II Corps, the 19th fought north. Much of the time spent in Sicily by the 19th Engineers was spent clearing mine fields that had been placed by German and Italian forces. Patton's armor columns had to have the mine fields cleared before they could advance. So, the 19th cleared paths for the tanks on a 24-hour basis.

*Unloading LST's at the Gela harbor, August 1943.*

The Allies continued to advance under heavy German and Italian fire from tanks, artillery and assault troops.

Berry watched as the 102d Airborne parachuted into Sicily and were shot while coming down.

The world watched during the next few weeks as Montgomery's British Eighth Army drove north from Syracuse to Messina against very heavy German and Italian fighting. Allied units were crushed from devastating Axis artillery and tank attacks. British forces were driven back time and time again, only to regroup and continue the drive.

*"Red Beach" at Gela Harbor, Sicily, when the men of the 19th Engineers came ashore, July 1943. Here the men are unloading engineer equipment and supplies from the assault craft. In the background, ships can be seen off shore.*

*Men of the 19th Engineers are clearing the harbor at Termini, Sicily, July 1943. The Germans had sunk ships and other craft in the harbor to keep the Allies from using it. Underwater explosives were used by the 19th to destroy the sunken ships.*

Meanwhile, Patton's Seventh Army, which was supposed to be guarding Montgomery's left flank, was instead driving to Palermo. Against orders, Patton was trying to steal the lime-light from Montgomery. His Seventh Army, which included the II Corps and the 19th Engineer Regiment was ordered to drive to Palermo and then, once Palermo was in Allied hands, to drive due East to Messina, and hopefully, to beat Montgomery there.

As Patton's Army drove toward Palermo, they continually met heavy German fighting reinforced by Italian and Sicilian units. Patton drove his units harder and harder and largely ignored his duty to guard Montgomery's left. Through the fighting, the 19th Engineers lead the way as they cleared mine fields and built bridges to allow infantry and armor units to continue the drive.

*Bailey bridge pieces stored for later use by the 19th Engineers in Sicily.*

As the 19th got closer to Palermo, Lt Berry was approached one day by a Lieutenant in the MP's who said that two of Berry's men were in jail. The two sergeants were seen by an American MP "molesting" a Sicilian woman and were jailed. Apparently, the woman had the biggest breasts either man had ever seen. They just couldn't help themselves and ran over and each one took turns pinching the woman's breasts. Berry went to the jail and had a chat with the head of the MP unit. He convinced the MP's to release the two men as they would be severely punished. Of course, they weren't.

When II Corps made it to Palermo with Patton in the lead, the crowds were in the streets welcoming the Americans. The 19th went through the streets with the other units and had a short time to rest before they continued to Messina. While there, an Italian man came up to Berry and with sign language told him that his family would like to have him to their house for a meal.

Berry went with the man to his house and was greeted by the man's family. They all sat down to dinner with pasta and what looked like small quail. Berry asked what the birds were and he was told that they

*German teller mines abandoned by retreating Nazi armies before they could be put to use. Thousands of mines similar to these were placed by German and Italian troops retreating toward Messina and were removed by the men of the 19th Engineer Regiment. (8.)*

were sparrows.

On the road from Palermo to Messina, the 19th continued to clear mines along the roads. One night during the drive to Messina, Captain Pohlmann and Lt. Berry went out to supervise clearing mines during the night. The 19th cleared mine fields 24 hours a day. F Company worked all night and the next morning Captain Pohlmann and Lt. Berry came back into camp with their men. When they arrived in camp, Lieutenants Ellis, Hanrahan, and Withers and their jeep driver beckoned Lt. Berry to go with them and the rest of F Company to continue the mine clearing operation. Lt. Berry wanted to go along, even though he had been out all night with Captain Pohlmann, but Captain Pohlmann refused to let him go. Instead, Captain Pohlmann explained that Lt Berry would have to get some rest so that he could go out again that night with the other half of F Company. So, the three lieutenants and their driver headed out to duty.

The Germans had blown a large bridge a few miles east of Nicosia near a town called Randazzo. As they typically did, they mined the by-pass routes on each side of the blown bridge. Although it was standard procedure to sweep both sides of a blown bridge, someone had not done a very good job. The jeep went around the bridge and hit a mine, killing all three men. Lt Ellis had been a close friend of Lt Berry and had been with the 19th since their days in Pasadena. Lts Wilson and Hanrahan were also close friends of Berry and were good officers. (1.)

One mine probably would not have killed all four men. The Germans often stacked mines on top of each other and this may have been the case. That incident badly depleted the officers of F Company, leaving only Captain Pohlmann and Lt. Berry.

*The three lieutenants of F Company, Charlie Ellis, Jerry Berry and Wilson Withers, taking a break during the battle for Sicily. Ellis and Withers were killed a few days later when a jeep they were in ran over a mine.*

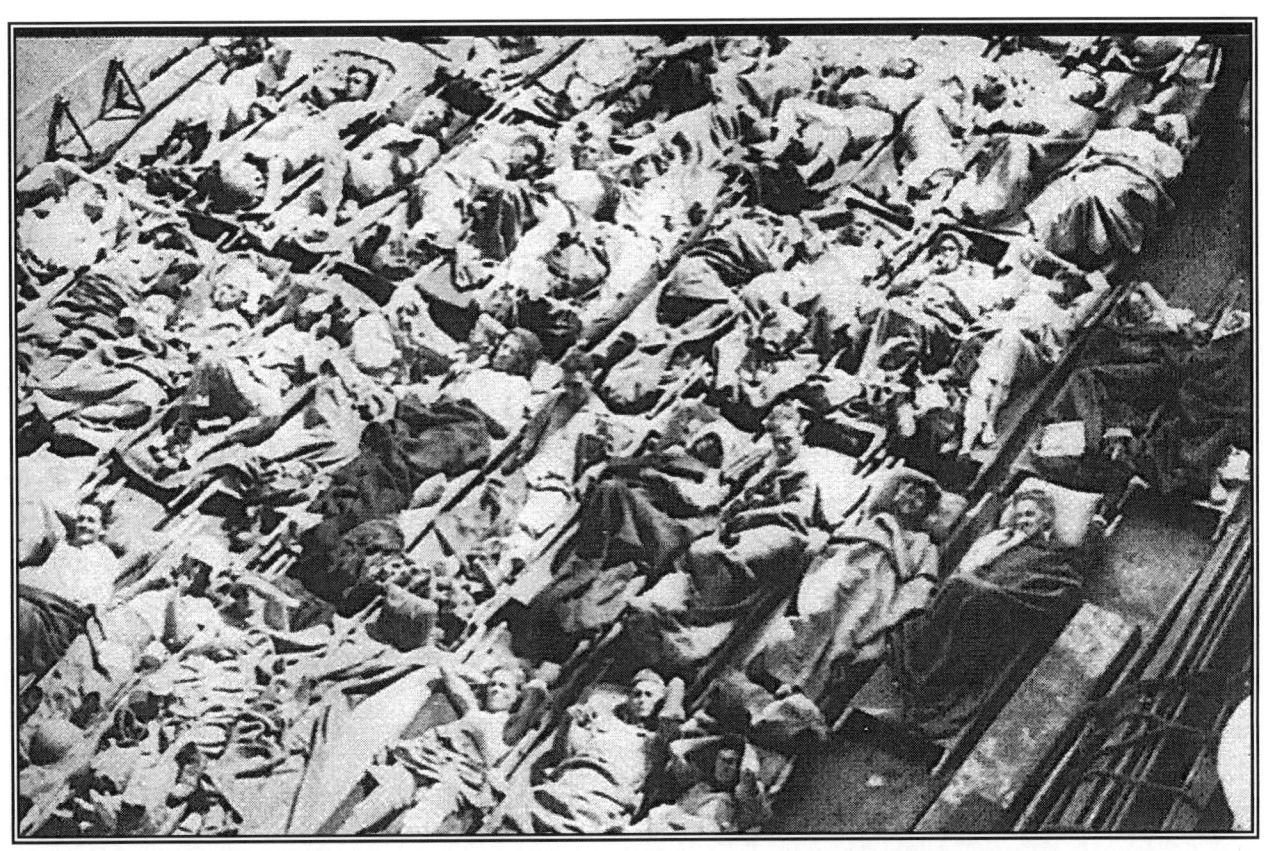

*Allied wounded were brought from the fighting zones back to bases where they were given immediate treatment. Here, wounded soldiers on stretchers cover the entire deck of a British landing craft in a Sicilian harbor. (8.)*

*Men of the US Seventh Army press on through Troina, Sicily. This town was a focal point of the German defense line in northern Sicily. (8.)*

*"Berry's Bridge" under construction by 3rd Platoon, F Company. At the time, it was the longest wooden bridge built by the Army. That's Lt Berry keeping a watchful eye in the foreground with a level and saw.*

On the fight to Messina, Lt Berry's platoon constructed the longest wooden bridge in Sicily bridging a road over a river. His platoon spent several days constructing the bridge. One evening as it was near dark, he noticed that many of his men had "disappeared". He went looking for the men and saw them all in line outside of the nearby railroad station. He walked up to the men and asked them what was going on and it was explained that there was a Sicilian woman inside "taking on all comers". Berry ordered the men back to work, much to the disappointment of those still in line that hadn't yet had their turn.

The next morning, Berry went looking for the Sicilian prostitute and brought her to the bridge site. When the men saw her in the daylight, they saw that she was an old woman with no teeth and very unattractive. At that point, all of the men who were denied their turn were glad for it and those who had a turn were nearly sick.

Fifth Army then turned east and took Messina – the gateway to Italy. The march from Palermo to Messina was rapid with little fighting as the Germans retreated quickly and got back to Italy.

During the last few days of the Sicilian Campaign, the 19th Engineers spent their days repairing bridges and clearing mines. Other elements of the 19th made ready for the forthcoming invasion of Italy. The Germans were gone and the Italians had signed an armistice with the Allies and had agreed to fight against the Germans. Days were also spent writing letters home and taking a few minutes here and there to relax.

*A wooden bridge being built by F Company, 19th Engineers in Sicily, August 1943.*

*Cpl Alphonso Rocco served as Lt Berry's jeep driver in North Africa and Sicily. He was from Ashtabula, Ohio, near Berry's hometown of Akron. Rocco was killed on September 5, 1943 in Empoli, Italy when his jeep ran over a mine.*

*Lt Berry on his "bridge" in Sicily. In the background, the train station can be seen that was used as a brothel during construction of the bridge.*

*Left to right, Staff Sgt Pittenger, Pfc Alfonso Rocco and Cpl Beale, taken at Conca, Italy, November 1943. Pfc Rocco was Berry's driver and was killed in Italy September 5, 1944.*

*American and British troops mop up snipers in Messina left behind to delay the advance of the Allies after the main body of Germans had fled to the Italian mainland, August 1943. (8.)*

*General Patton, commander of 7th Army, in Sicily. (11.)*

*Troop ships filled to the brim with men and equipment heading toward landing areas in Italy.(4.)*

*Lt. Berry and Sgt Pittenger with a Sicilian buddy.*

# Invasion of Italy

Following the conquest of Sicily, a number of changes were made to the Allied command structure as well as that of the Axis powers. After Sicily fell, Mussolini was ousted as the leader of Italy and in September, the new Italian government signed an armistice with the Allies and joined them against Germany. This treachery, of course, infuriated Hitler who was, by now, used to experiencing defeat and watching his Axis powers disintegrate. Rommel had been recalled to Germany and was soon sent to France to plan for the German defense of the European mainland when the Allies invaded in northern

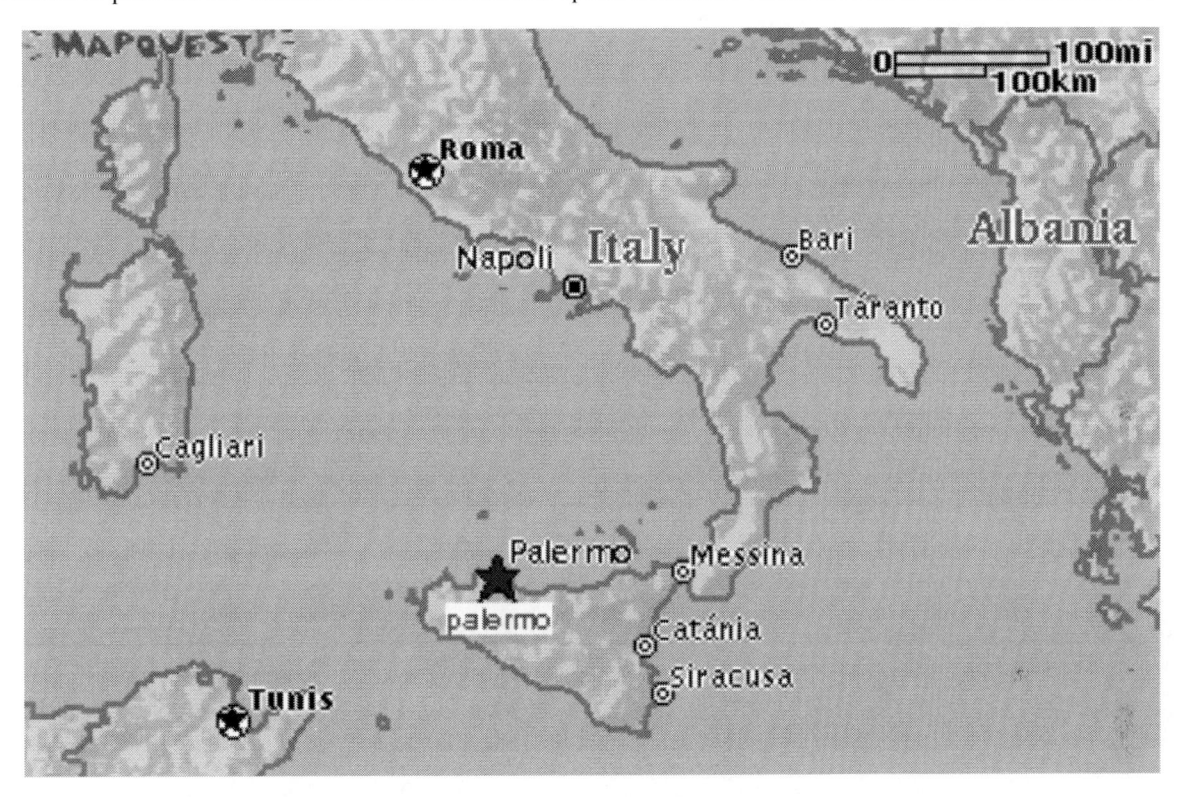

France. When Italy surrendered in September, Hitler took personal command of the Italian campaign and assigned both Field Marshall Rommel and Field Marshall Kesselring as his field commanders. Rommel was assigned to the defense of northern Italy and Kesselring, the south.

Both commanders knew that the invasion of Italy would happen very soon and that it would come up the Italian boot. Rommel argued to Hitler that the best strategy was to withdraw completely from southern Italy to the Po River north of Rome and to establish strong defenses that would maximize the resources of the German army and would allow for safer and shorter supply lines from Germany. However, Kesselring argued to hold the Allied advance in the south, to hold Rome and to prevent the Allies from taking any ground. In addition, Kesselring argued, that if the Germans withdrew to the Po River, Allied bombers could be based in Italy close enough to bomb the center of Germany. He also argued that the mountains of southern Italy were superb for defending against the Allies.

Hitler considered both positions during September of 1943 and, as he detested giving up one square yard of his Reich, he eventually ordered the defense of southern Italy according to Kesselring's plan.(5.)

Also on the Axis side, General Frido von Senger was transferred from the Russian front, where he proved

*Lt. Gen Mark Clark, commander of the US Fifth Army in Italy. (12.)*

himself as a great and brave officer, to command the 14th Panzer Corps in southern Italy under Field Marshall Kesselring. He had commanded the 14th Panzer Corps in Sicily and now had retreated to southern Italy where he was planning the forward defenses of the Italian boot. The 14th Panzer Corps now consisted of close to 75,000 men in five divisions and was spread across the south of Italy to stop the Allies.

Meanwhile, General Eisenhower was sent to England to prepare for the Allied invasion of France scheduled for the spring of 1944. General Patton, who had commanded the II Corps in North Africa and then, the US Seventh Army in Sicily, got in hot water for the infamous slapping of the corporal in the medical tent in Sicily. After the fighting in Sicily, Seventh Army was disbanded and Patton was also sent to England to command a fake army being constructed out of plywood by the same camouflage unit Berry had first been assigned to in California.

General Omar Bradley, who had commanded II Corps in Sicily under Patton's Seventh Army, was also assigned to England to help Eisenhower with planning the Normandy invasion. Bradley was replaced by Major General Geoffrey Keyes who took command of II Corps. The 19th Engineer Regiment (Combat) stayed as an element of II Corps.

British General Sir Harold Alexander was the overall Allied commander for the Italian invasion. He had Montgomery's British Eighth Army and the newly formed American Fifth Army which was now commanded by 47-year-old Lieutenant General Mark Clark. Fifth Army was composed of a hodge-podge of Allied units, including divisions from India, New Zealand, Poland, France, Tunisia, Algeria, Morocco, Great Britain and, the United States II Corps.

It was decided by the Allies to invade Italy from the south and to fight northerly to Rome and on into Austria and Germany. The fighting in Italy would open another front that would force Germany to continue to send units that could otherwise be used to fight the advancing Russians in the east or to defend against the inevitable invasion of Normandy.

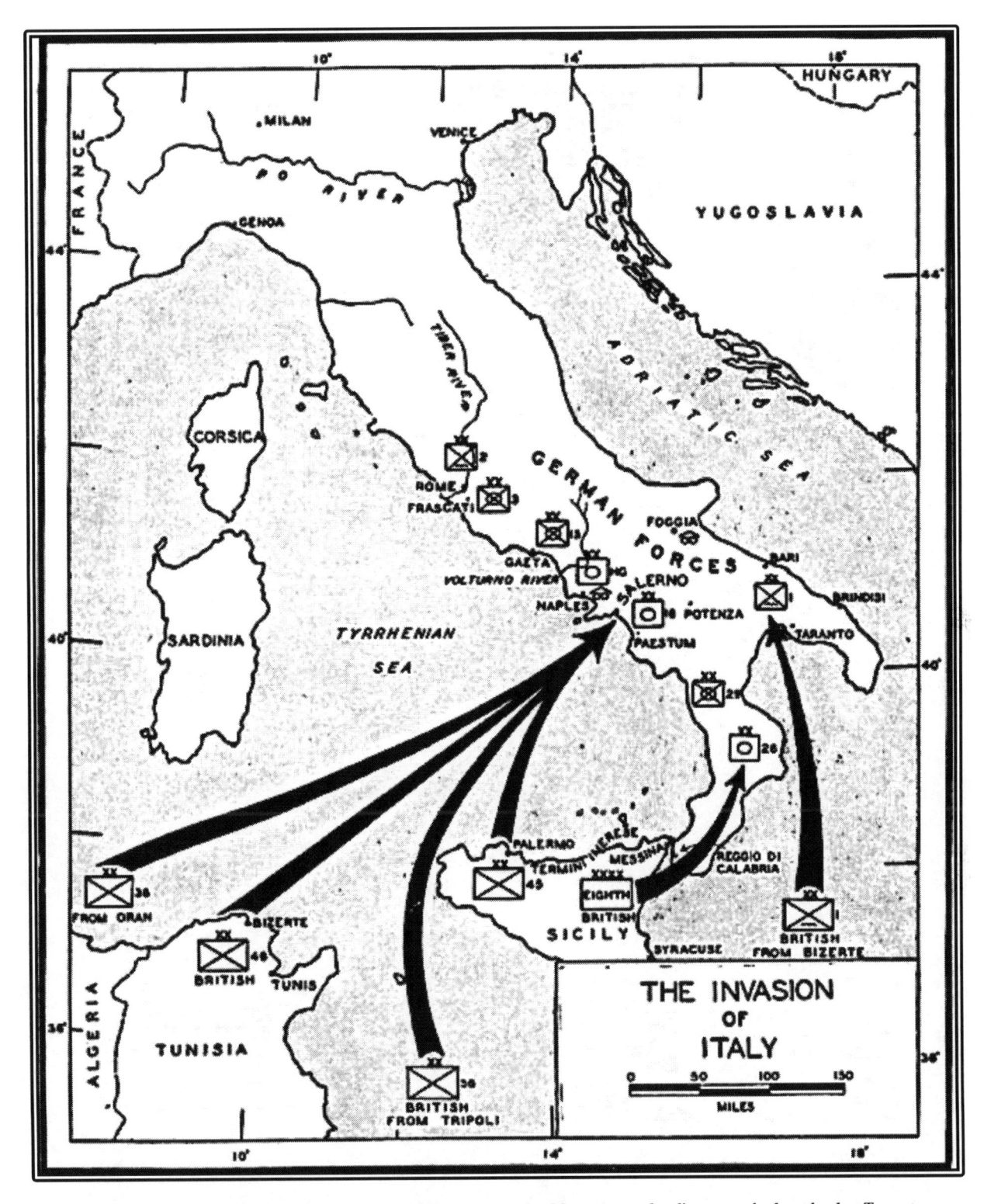

*The invasion of Italy, showing the British Eight Army under Montgomery landing near the boot heel at Taranto in the east and the American Fifth Army under General Clark landing at Salerno, just south of Naples. The British Eighth Army Group, which included some elements of II Corps as well as some elements of the 19th Engineers, landed at Reggio Calabria, in the center. Berry and his unit was with the British landing at Reggio Calabria.*

*Canadian forces land near Reggio Calabria, Italy, near Messina, Sicily, near where the 19th Engineers landed in southern Italy.*

*The British Eighth Army landing at Reggio Calabria in southern Italy on September 3, 1943, near where the 19th Engineers landed.*

No army in history had been successful in conquering Italy from the south. (5.) Hannibal had crossed the Alps and invaded from the north in order to avoid fighting through the rugged mountains that run the length of Italy. There are only three roads that can be used to move an army north to Rome from the southern Italian boot.

The road in the east runs along the Adriatic Sea and sweeps well east of Rome next to rugged mountains and impassable valleys. The western route runs along the Tyrrhenian Sea and narrows so badly in some places to make it impossible as the main route of travel by an army. The only feasible route to Rome is up present day Route 6 through the mountain passes and through the Liri River valley. Route 6 in 1943 was, essentially, the Appian Way, originally built by the Romans in the first century. Both the Allied and Axis armies knew this was the only feasible route to Rome and both planned accordingly.

*F Company mess kitchen near Mignano, Italy, December 1943.*

General Alexander and his staff developed a plan to try to draw the Germans away from the route that the Allies planned to use through Naples. Alexander sent elements of the British Eighth Army under Montgomery to land at the Gulf of Taranto on the east side of the boot in order to pull German units away from the strength of the German line in Naples. The feint did not work.

The British landed at Reggio Calabria in the Gulf of Taranto and met heavy resistance but Kesselring did not move any of his units from the Naples area. On September 9th, Fifth Army under Mark Clark, including elements of II Corps, landed on the west coast of Italy south of Salerno. Kesselring put Senger's 14th Panzer Corps to oppose the Allies' Fifth Army and at the same time sent in German troops and forced labor units composed of Italians and Africans, among others, to construct the Gustav Line which was to be the "final" defensive position of the German army.

As the US Fifth Army landed in Salerno, the British Eighth Army was slugging it out southeast of Salerno at Reggio and was advancing north up the toe of the Italian boot. Elements of Fifth Army, including units of II Corps and including Company F of the 19th Engineers, was with the British Eighth Army at Reggio. Lt. Berry and his platoon, therefore, fought north up the toe while other elements of Fifth Army were landing at Salerno.

The 19th Engineers were assigned to support infantry divisions and loaded their men and equipment onto ships and crossed the short distance to Italy. F Company of the 19th rather than land at Salerno, crossed the Straits of Messina to Italy and advanced up the toe of the boot toward Naples following in the steps of the British Eighth Army who had preceded them. All along the way from Naples to Cassino, the 19th cleared mines in front of the advancing Allies. Fighting was fierce as the Germans retreated.

Allied air forces, including both British and American squadrons, supported both prongs of the Allied attack. The air forces were successful in nearly destroying the German Luftwaffe which afforded protection to both landings and to beachhead operations. When the landings at Salerno took place on September 9th, the German 10th Corps reacted quickly to throw their weight at the Allied forces and attempted to drive them back to the sea. After several days of vicious fighting, the German forces made an organized withdrawal north to the outskirts of Naples.

*Bridge destroyed by the retreating Germans in southern Italy, October 1943.*

The Allied forces needed the port of Naples to supply its armies with ammunition, supplies and replacements. The Germans were determined to hold Naples long enough to destroy as much of the harbor as possible. In order to slow the Allied progress, the Germans placed mines throughout the route to Naples and destroyed every bridge as it retreated to Naples. Almost every mine was booby-trapped.

As the Allies advanced toward Naples, engineer units, including the 19th Engineers, were out in front of the advancing columns to clear paths through the mine fields and to rebuild bridges so that Allied tanks and trucks could pass. As bridges were rebuilt, the 19th was faced with a continuous need for bridging materials. Bailey bridge pieces were desperately needed and had to be shipped from Sicily or North Africa, unloaded at Salerno or Reggio, and transported by truck to the front where the 19th would rebuild the bridges destroyed by the retreating Germans. Tons of Bailey bridge pieces, lumber, bolts, decking material, and material for foundations and abutments were needed. Often, the 19th would build bridges while under fire.

Pontoon bridges were also used to allow both troops and vehicles to cross rivers along the advance. Pontoon bridges "floated" by using rubber rafts or wooden pontoons to support wooden treadways. Pedestrian pontoon bridges also allowed infantry to cross rivers but also provided easy targets for German infantry, mortar units or snipers.

*Engineers repair and rebuild a destroyed bridge in order to keep supplies and troops moving north up the Italian boot. Here they are completing a double-double Bailey bridge over treacherous currents of the Volturno River. (12.) A Bailey bridge built with double-high sides is designed to for tanks to cross.*

*Vehicles are unloaded at the Paestum beaches, just south of Salerno in southern Italy. This landing craft, or LST, helped the Allies land supplies, men, vehicles and weapons. (12.)*

*19th Engineer officers, Lt Gillis, Lt Prestridge and Cpt Klabunde, near Venafro, Italy, January 1944.*

Men of the 19th Engineers worked day and night to construct bypasses around blown bridges and to build temporary bridges for men and vehicles to cross.

By late September 1943, Fifth Army was poised to enter Naples while the Germans were hurriedly destroying as much of the harbor as they could. Finally, on October 1, 1943, the leading elements of Fifth Army captured Naples. The city was badly bombed and battered. German demolitions had taken a heavy toll as they had blasted water lines, electrical plants and generally destroyed the utility systems supporting the harbor.(12.)

Engineer units began immediately to rebuild the port as the Fifth Army continued its advance north to Rome. The next obstacle was the Volturno River where the Germans had decided to make a stand. Again, the 19th Engineer Regiment would be called upon to help breach the river by building floating pontoon bridges while under savage fire from the Germans on the north side of the Volturno. By October 6th, Fifth Army was aligned on the south side of the Volturno and ready for a coordinated attack across the river. Across the river, the Germans were well entrenched on high ground looking down on the American forces who had to advance without cover.

*A revetment being built by 3rd Platoon, F Company, near Mignano, Italy, December 1943.*

October 12th and 13th was scheduled to be the all-out attack to cross the Volturno. Preceding that date, engineer units had scouted crossing points and had assembled bridge equipment making ready for their task. At 8:00 at night on October 12th, Allied artillery opened up all along the 40-mile length of the Volturno River with both high explosive rounds as well as smoke rounds to help hide the activities of the men crossing the river.

Elements of various infantry divisions used rafts and boats to cross the river in the darkness and with smoke cover, secured beachheads on the north bank. As soon as the beachheads were secure, engineer units began to assemble pontoon bridges to allow more men and vehicles to cross.

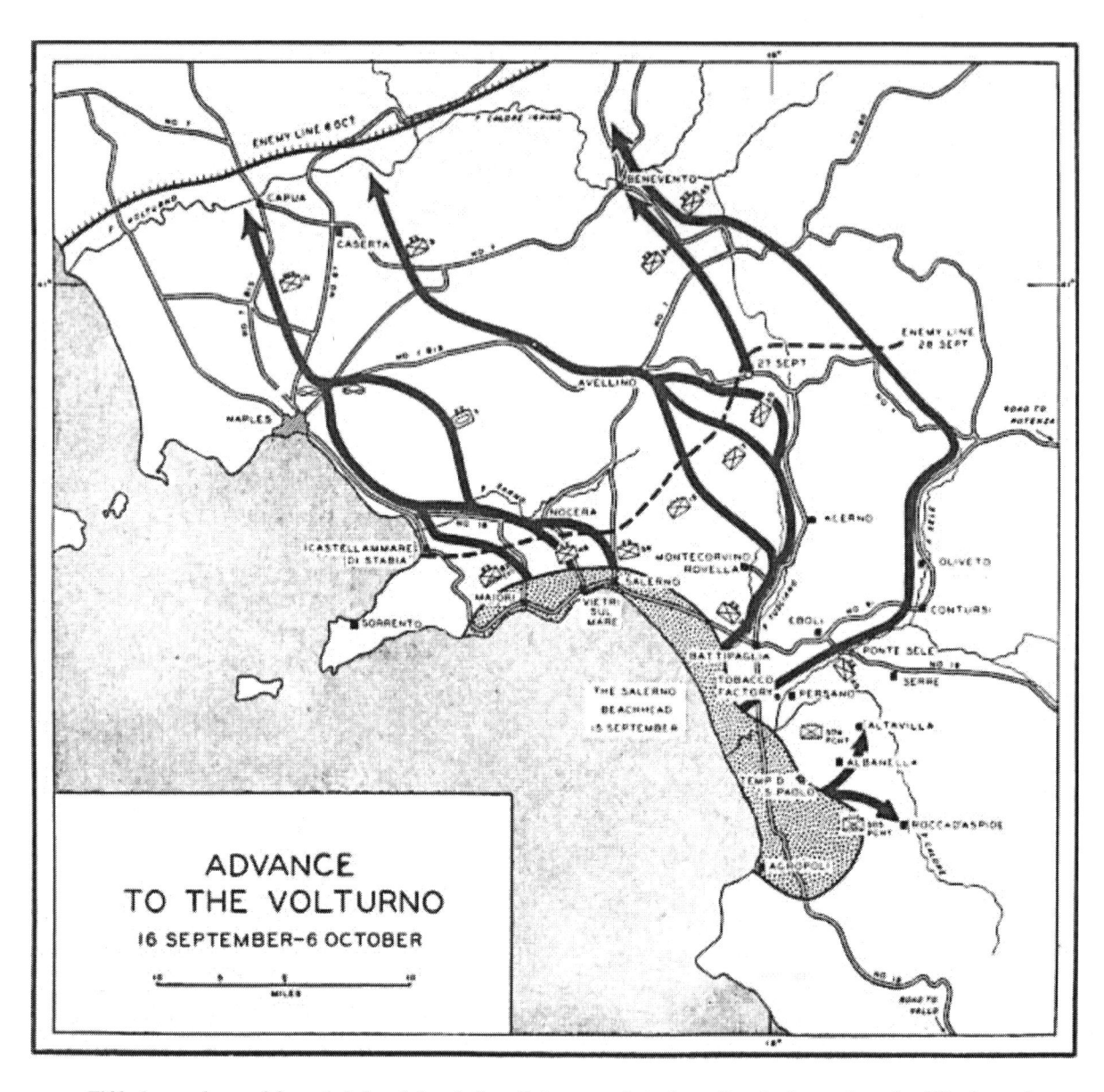

*Fifth Army advanced from their beach heads from Salerno south to Agropli and advanced north of Naples and to the Volturno River where the Germans had established a devensive line.*

*Elements of the 19th Engineers using a raft to ferry troops and vehicles across the Volturno River, October, 1943.*
*(12.)*

*American infantry crossing a pontoon bridge constructed by Berry's 3rd Platoon, F Company, December 1943 on the Volturno River, just northeast of Caserta, near Limatola, Italy.*

*US Infantry move to the front in the Venafro sector in southern Italy. The men of F Company later built a road on this same trail in January 1944. (12.)*

Cpt Ed Pohlmann, Lt D'Ambrosi, Lt Berry, Maj Lamb, Cpt Bartlett, Cpt Steffa, at the 19th Engineer bivouac site near Miganano, Italy December 1943. At this time, the Allies were driving north up the Italian boot, toward the Germans dug in along the Gustav Line.

*F Company constructing an experimental treadway bridge carried by a tank, March 1944. (12.)*

*F Company camp near Mignano, Italy, December 1943.*

A certain kind of bridge called a "treadway" bridge was used at several locations. Whole sections of bridge and decking were assembled on the south side of the river and were then floated into place.

As the Allies advanced and the Germans retreated, the temporary pontoon bridges were replaced by Bailey Bridges which were assembled by engineer units and put in place where destroyed bridges had been. In other places, bypasses or "shoe-flies" were also constructed to enable light vehicles to cross quickly.

As October turned to November, the winter rains came as did colder days and nights. Rain turned the unpaved roads of southern Italy into mud slides. Vehicles of all kinds were constantly getting stuck in mud and the men of Fifth Army got to know the mud very well. They slept in it, ate in it, walked in it and sat in it. They were altogether miserable as they fought the Germans, the wet, the cold and the relentless pressure to move north.

*Staff Sergeant Locke, at the Tori railhead, Italy, January 1944.*

The Allied forces pressed on toward the towns of Mignano and Venafro. By November 17th, II Corps had been brought on line. At that time, General Clark had 10th Corps on the left, II Corps on left-center; VI Corps on right-center; and the 34th and 45th Infantry Divisions on his right. In front of them was the German 10th Corps, the Herman Goering Division and Senger's 14th Panzer Corps along the Gustav Line defending some of the roughest terrain in Europe. During November, Fifth Army consolidated and secured forward positions while the constant logistics of bringing supplies, reinforcements, vehicles, ammunition and gasoline to the front caught up with the advancing Allies.

In late November, Lt. Berry and his platoon were near San Pietro clearing mines when they were shelled by German artillery. His jeep was hit and he lost his right front wheel. Throughout November and December 1943, the 19th Engineer Regiment was spread along the front of the advancing II Corps. They worked day and night to build bridges and clear mine fields placed by the retreating Germans. In most cases, mine fields are covered by fire so casualties are expected when clearing a mine field.

*Master Sergeant Bassett near the Tori Railhead in southern Italy, January 1944.*

Italians never seemed to have their heart in the war, especially to fight the Americans. The Germans made the Italians place many of the mines. However, many of the Italians would place the mines with the pins still in place so that they would not explode. As the engineers would remove a mine, they would immediately remove the fuse so that it would not explode. In one case, one engineer soldier with the 19th, forgot to remove the fuse and put the mine in the back of a truck. As more and more mines were taken out of the ground and placed in the back of the truck, the weight on top of the fused mine grew. Finally, enough weight was on top of the fuse so that it exploded, along with the other mines. The explosion wounded or killed 13 members of the 19th Engineers.

*This was my S/Sgt in E Co. S/SGT FAULKNER — now 1st Sgt. I had my picture taken the same day — I was right there with this detail — see letter from april 5-20th/1944.*

19th ENGRS

Teller mines like these were planted by the thousands along Italy's beaches.

***Staff Sergeant Faulkner of E Company, 19th Engineer Regiment stacking a teller mine removed by the engineers from the beaches of southern Italy, April, 1944. Notice Berry's hand-written comments made in late 1944 when this booklet was published. (12.)***

*Entertainers like comedian Joe E. Brown stopped by the 19th Engineers to say hello during the Italian campaign.*

*Captain Mewshaw signing up to be a WAC escort on R&R with Cpt Berry at Minturno Beach, Italy.*

By January 15th, Fifth Army was deployed from the Tyhrennian Sea in the west to the British Eighth Army in the center of Italy and along the Rapido River in front of the Gustav line.

The Gustav Line ran across southern Italy for about 50 miles through some of the most rugged mountains in Europe. General Senger knew that the Allies would come up the center of the boot through the Liri Valley and into the center of the Gustav Line as this was the only feasible route.

The Germans left mines everywhere they could in order to stop or slow the Allies. Most mines that were left were anti-tank mines however many were also anti-personnel mines. Many of the mines were booby-trapped to make them much more dangerous to remove.

After the landing in Italy, the Allies advanced north up the Italian boot toward the Gustav Line built by Kesselring to stop them. Kesselring's strategy was to slow the Allies' advance by using mines, blowing bridges and defending tough terrain in order to buy time to strengthen the defenses of the Gustav Line. In the center of the Line, the Liri River valley runs next to Monte Cassino, a mountain top with a fantastic view down the Liri River valley and across the Rapido River. At the bottom of the mountain runs the Rapido River which flows into the Liri.

Sheer fatigue is registered by this soldier who has just returned from carrying supplies to his comrades fighting on a mountain top.

*An American soldier taking a break after carrying supplies to his unit fighting nearby on an Italian mountain top. Winter 1944. (12.)*

*3rd Platoon, F Company, breaking rock with a jackhammer near Mignano, Italy, December 1943.*

*A railroad line repaired by F Company, near St. Remy, Italy.*

*Crossing the Volturno River by raft, January 1944.*

*Trucks are crossing this floating Bailey bridge built across the Volturno River near Capua Italy, built by the 19th Engineers during the advance toward Cassino, November 1943. The rafts supporting the center of the bridge were floated into place and secured with cables prior to building the roadway and decking.*

# The Battle of Monte Cassino

In October and November, as the Allies advanced along both prongs up the boot toward the Gustav Line, the Germans were helping the monastery at Monte Cassino to box up their sacred manuscripts and art and to transport it north to Rome. The Abbey of Monte Cassino is one of the most sacred sites in Christianity. In the year 529, the wandering Saint Benedict chose this mountain top to found the monastery which bears his name. Over the centuries, the Abbey of Monte Cassino grew to be the largest and most important of Western monasteries. The abbey was a powerful voice in the Roman Catholic Church and was a center for art, learning and Christianity for centuries. Over the centuries, the abbey expanded and a basilica and cathedral were built on the site. The abbey was beautifully adorned with tapestries, statues, frescoes and paintings, as well as centuries of hand-written manuscripts. (5.)

The abbey overlooks the Rapido and Liri Valleys as well as the town of Cassino of 25,000 and was at the crossroads of the main route to Rome through the Gustav line. It was plain to all that the treasures of the abbey and the abbey itself were in danger. Hitler ordered the Herman Goering Division to relocate the treasures of the abbey to safe keeping at the Vatican and the unit worked throughout October, November

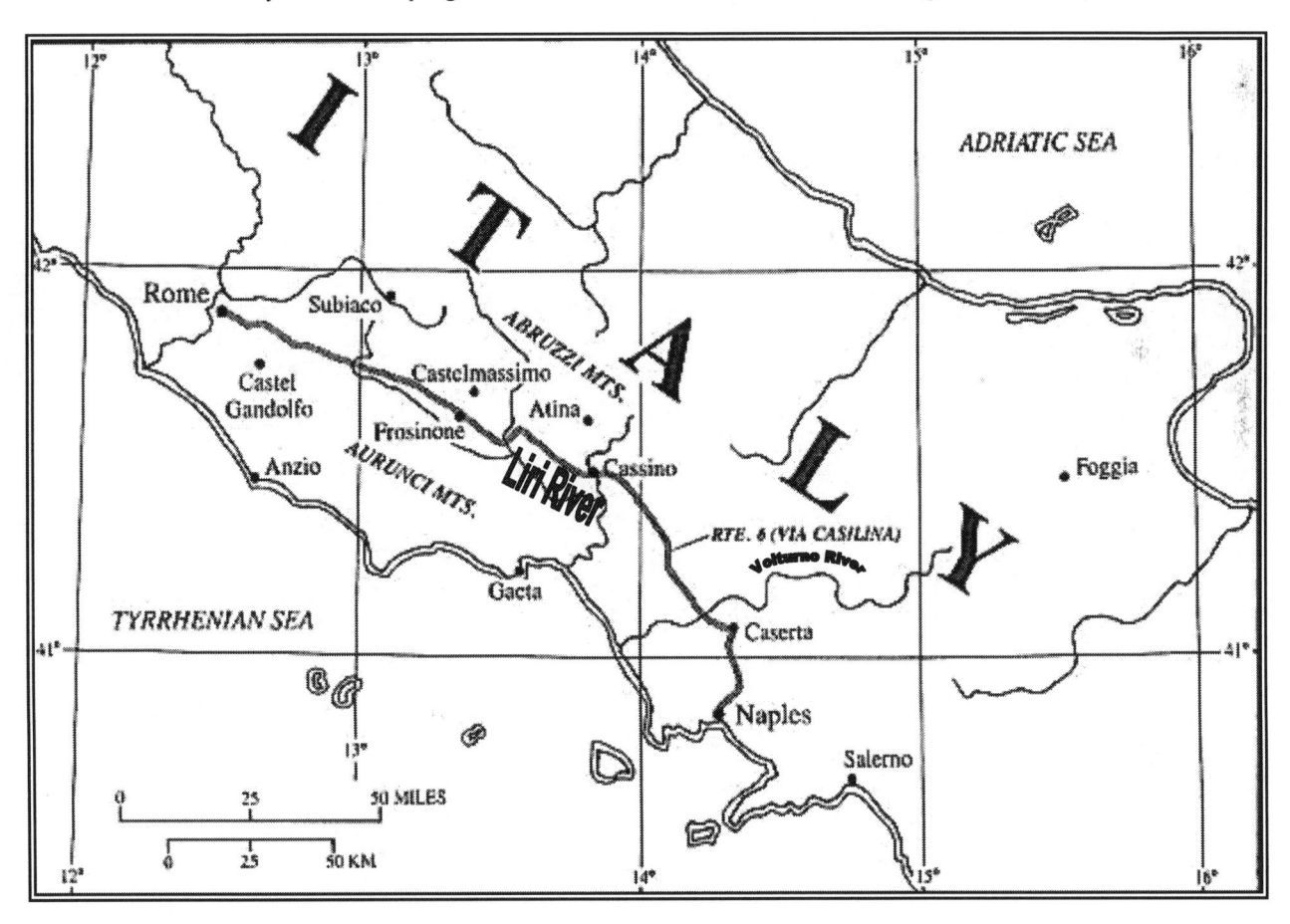

*Central Italy showing the route in the Liri River Valley from Naples to Rome. Also shown is the town of Cassino and the Volturno River.*

and December of 1943 to crate and transport the treasures to Rome while the Allies were advancing toward the abbey. Many of the crates and boxes from the abbey never made it to Rome but were, instead, shipped to Herman Goering himself as well as other senior Nazi officials. Some of the artifacts have never been recovered.

As the artifacts were being transported to Rome, General Senger was strengthening his positions around the abbey and on adjacent hill tops and was preparing for the inevitable arrival of Mark Clark's Fifth Army. Artillery and tank emplacements were strategically located while mortar and machine gun units were positioned all along the crests of hills and mountains around the abbey area. Below, in the Rapido and Liri River valleys, dams were broken so that waters from the rivers would flood the surrounding flat lands making it nearly impossible to drive through the area with wheeled vehicles.

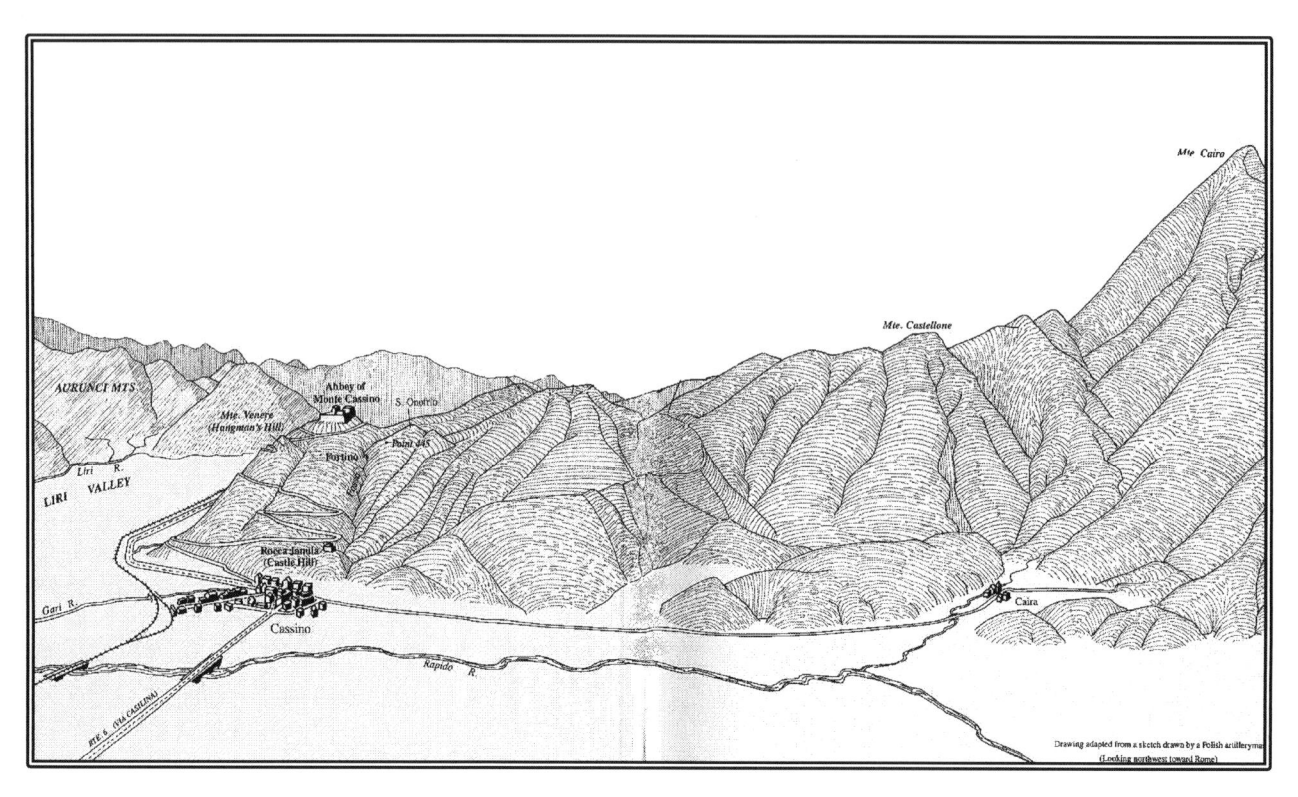

*The Monte Cassino area in profile. The Rapido River runs east-west in front of Cassino. (5.)*

There were a lot of caves in the hills around the mountain top which were soon occupied by German units who established mortar and artillery positions outside of the caves so that when they came under fire, they could quickly find shelter in a cave and then emerge as soon as the shelling stopped and continue to fire on Allied troops. General Senger surveyed his positions daily and made corrections and strengthened lines of fire, awaiting the advancing Allied soldiers.

The Catholic Church met frequently with the German army and insisted that the Germans not occupy the abbey for fear that it would bring destruction by Allied artillery and bombers. Finally in December, Kesselring specifically ordered Senger not to occupy the abbey but the Germans cleverly continued to occupy the area immediately around the abbey. As the Allies advanced north, refugees poured into the abbey to find safety and shelter from the bombing and artillery that was happening to the south. In addition, local Italian workers continued to assist the Germans by making crates and boxes in which to transport artifacts to the Vatican.

On December 19, 1943, the Allies started bombing the areas around the abbey but took great care to avoid the abbey itself. Roosevelt had declared that the Allies would take extreme care to avoid destruction of Italian monuments, cathedrals and historical shrines as Italy was now its ally. The Germans, of course, knew this and continually used that fact to their advantage.

By mid-January 1944, the Allies had taken Naples and had pushed to the Gustav Line and were in position to make the first thrust to take Monte Cassino. General Clark conceived a plan to attack the Rapido River and Liri River valleys while simultaneously landing a force behind the Axis lines along the west coast of Italy at Anzio.

The attack across the Rapido has become known as the Battle of the Rapido. It ended up being the most painful defeat of the Allies in the European theater during the entire war.

*The Express Highway leading into Cassino, Italy, January 1944.*

The crossing of the Rapido was to take place at three points. The first attack, was to be made by the British on the right flank, and was meant to be a diversion and to draw fire and troops in that direction while the main attack occurred on the left.

The second attack was also to be made by the British as they crossed the Rapido southwest of Monte Cassino and was meant to take the heights across from the Liri Valley to protect the main thrust by the Americans who would cross in the center near Sant' Angelo.

In this way, the first attack would protect the main American attack to their right and the second attack would protect the American left while the Americans crossed the Rapido in force and attacked Monte Cassino itself. The 19th Engineers was ordered to support the American attack by constructing bridges and pontoon crossings of the Rapido River to allow infantry units and vehicles to quickly cross the river.

Engineer units were ordered to bring bridging equipment to the front and to begin to prepare the southern banks of selected crossing areas for the eventual attack. F Company was assigned certain crossing sites near San Angelo, a little west of the town of Cassino.

*Lt Berry and Cpt Ed Pohlman, southern Italy, near Cassino January 1944.*

The first attack occurred on January 17th and caught the Germans by surprise. The British captured the town of Minturno and established a beachhead on the north side of the river.

General Senger, however, arrived on the scene and realized quickly that this was not the main attack and did not move additional German troops to support his units there. Instead he called Kesselring and requested two divisions which were being held in reserve near Anzio. Kesselring agreed and sent the units to support Senger and to stop the British attack. Senger was therefore ready and waiting when the Allies launched their second attack to the southwest on January 19th. He anticipated the second and third attacks and repositioned his best troops to oppose the Allied thrust.

The second attack, also lead by the British, occurred on the night of January 18th in the fog. The river was running very swift and few men were able to cross. Those that did were under heavy fire and were not able to take the heights on the north side of the Rapido and the British commander quickly called off the attack and withdrew his men.

*Pontoon foot bridge built by 3rd Platoon, F Company, probably over the Rapido River near San Angelo in southern Italy, 1943. These bridges were very common and the men of the 19th got very good at building them in a hurry. These bridges allowed infantry units to cross quickly. However, there was little cover for racing infantry men when they crossed. Larger bridges were built later once beachheads were secured on the other side of the river.*

The center attack, led by the US Fifth Army, was spearheaded by the 36th Infantry Division, a Texas National Guard unit, and supported by the 19th Engineers of II Corps. The ground on the south side of the river was like a swamp as it had been flooded earlier by the Germans. Vehicles broke down and slid off of roads and bogged down in heavy mud, which made it difficult to get men on line on time.

The Germans had also cut down trees and brush on the south side of the Rapido to allow them to have clear fields of fire. Artillery and mortar units were zeroed on expected assembly points and the Germans were dug in and waiting.

The Rapido itself was around 50-feet wide and was from 5 to 10 feet deep, making it too deep to wade or drive across. The current moved very fast at around 8 miles per hour and was very cold in that winter in January. At the proposed main crossing at San Angelo, the Germans were dug-in into trenches and had machine gun posts and infantry units all along the north side of the crossing. Finally, the river was heavily mined on both sides of the river bank and barbed wire made it more difficult to maneuver.

The main thrust across the Rapido at San Angelo took place on January 20, 1944. The night before, on January 19th, the 19th Engineers brought up bridge pieces and rafts for the crossing. The engineers were to sweep the mines at the selected river crossing sites and the infantry units were to cross by boat or raft and once the other side was secured, the engineers were to construct footbridges on pontoons to allow the rest of the infantry to cross. Finally, after the Germans were pushed further back, the engineers would construct Bailey bridges to allow for trucks, half-tracks and tanks to cross to support the advancing infantry and smash the Gustav Line.

However, as the first wave of infantry went to cross the river in their rafts and boats, it was discovered that during the night, many of the boats and rafts were destroyed by artillery and machine gun fire. This prevented many of the men from crossing and the few who did were not able to fight their way far from the river bank. Others were killed and disabled by the mines and the heavy fire from the embedded Germans. As a result, the 19th Engineers were not able to construct footbridges. By 4:00 in the morning on the 20th only one footbridge had been built and that one was wet, slippery and difficult to get across. By dawn only around 450 men had crossed the Rapido and, since neither of their flanks had been secured by the British, they continued to experience heavy fire and mounting casualties.

Mark Clark ordered the attack continued but few other Americans were able to cross the Rapido to help those who had crossed. The Bailey bridges could not be built by the engineers who were under heavy fire as they continued to try to bridge the river with mortar, artillery, machine gun and rifle fire raining down

*This "treadway" bridge built by the 19th Engineers across the Volturno enabled tanks and vehicles to continue the push north. (12.)*

on them. Without the support of tanks, the men on the north side of the Rapido were doomed. Those that were not killed or captured swam back across the Rapido and the attack was called off on January 22nd. In the three days, there were 1,681 Americans dead, wounded or missing.

F Company of the 19th was given the mission to support the 36th Infantry Division and to build footbridges and Bailey bridges across the Rapido at San Angelo. In addition, the 19th's mission was to clear mines in the path of the advancing assault troops and to build bridges to allow troops and equipment to get in position to continue the assault.

As Berry remembers, "the Germans were on one side of the river and we were on the other side. We would sing one verse of 'Lili Marlene' and they would sing the next verse." The Germans' line included interlaced railroad ties holding earth embankments forming redoubts. The line was very well defended and stiff."

On January 19, 1944, Lt Berry led his unit near San Angelo, Italy and was ordered to clear mines around the assault areas, build a footbridge across the Rapido River once infantry units were across and then to build a Bailey bridge to allow vehicles and tanks to cross. Berry and his platoon approached the river and began to clear the mines near the bridge head. As the assault troops tried to cross the river, 3rd Platoon tried to construct a footbridge. They would assemble the footbridge about three hundred yards from the river and would then take the footbridge by boat upstream to the bridgehead.

*An American tank bogged down in the Rapido River valley, January 1944. The Germans flooded the Rapido River valley to prevent vehicles from driving toward their waiting lines. (12.)*

The trip to the bridge head was done under fire as men would try to fight back while holding the foot bridge, paddling and firing at the same time. When they got to the bridge head, they would try to secure the section of footbridge on the south side of the river then push the whole footbridge across the river. The man in front of the boat would then try to secure the footbridge to something on the other side. Time after time, the man in the front would be shot and the bridge would then float back down the river. The platoon tried over and over again before finally securing the bridge to the other side. Several men were lost in the action.

Although the Battle of the Rapido ended on January 22nd, the Battle of Monte Cassino continued for four more months. The battle of the Rapido River was one of the largest defeats suffered by the U.S. Army during World War II and, after the war, was the subject of an investigation in 1946 by the Congress to establish responsibility for the disaster.

The 19th Engineers continued to clear mines and to secure bridgehead sites. The F Company 3rd Platoon bridge head was covered by fire from the Germans and one night mortar fire rained on the group. On January 31st, Lt Berry was at the front helping his men clear mines when one mortar round landed near Berry detonating a mine as it exploded. Berry got both shell fragments and mine fragments in his head and face. He received facial lacerations and was deafened for a time.

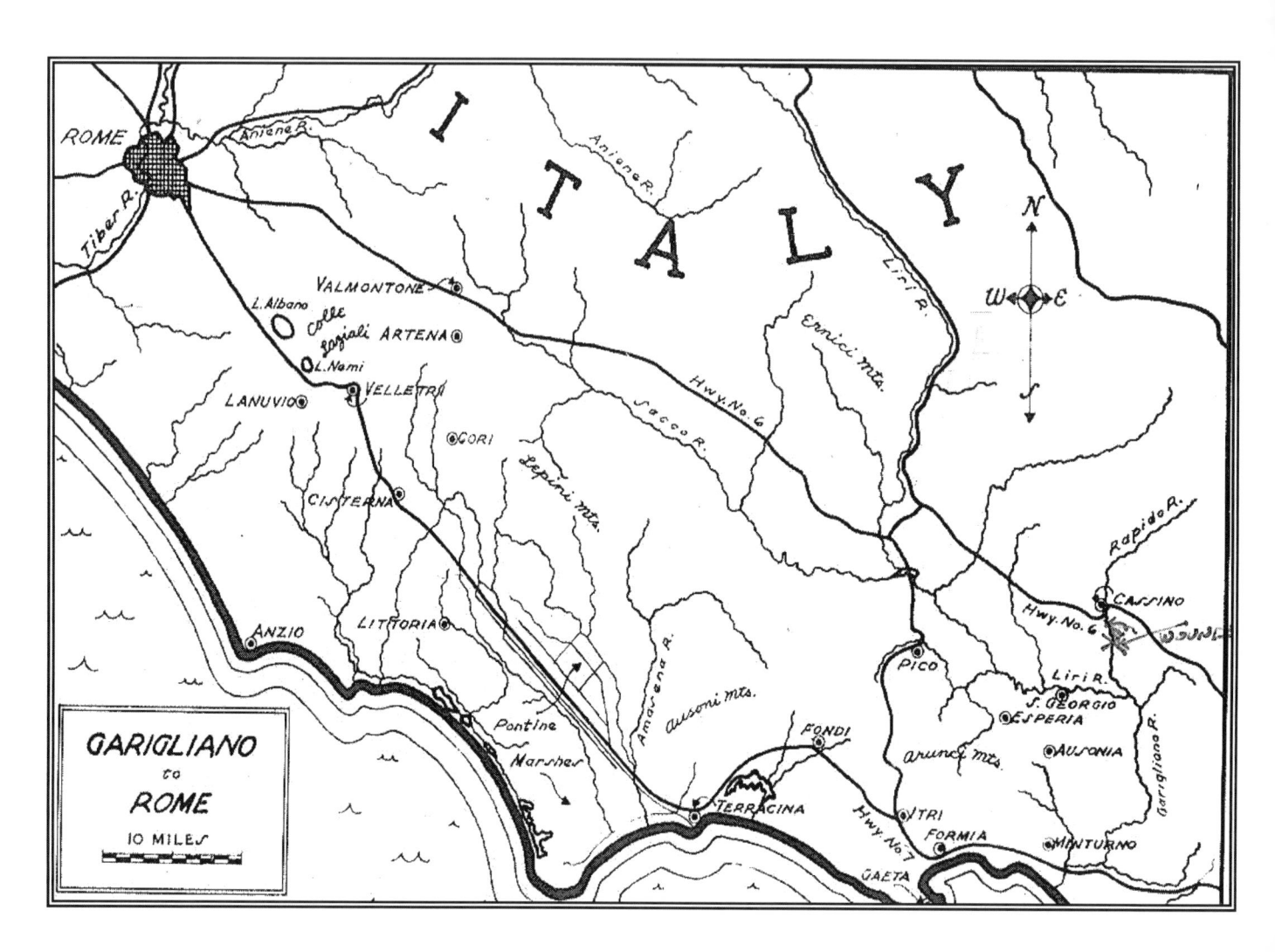

*Central Italy showing Highway 6 through Cassino and through the Liri Valley to Rome. Anzio is shown just above the legend box on the southern coast of Italy.*

*Litter bearers bring back wounded during attempt to span the Rapido River near Cassino, Italy." 23 January 1944*

*The 19th Engineer motor pool under camouflage nets, Italy 1944.*

*1st Sgt Ray Palmquist, F Company, Mignano, Italy, Jan. 1944. Sgt Palmquist was killed later in the war.*

After being wounded, Berry was sent to Naples to an Army hospital where the shell fragments were removed and he recovered for about two weeks. He received the Purple Heart for being wounded in action. After being treated, he returned to duty and his unit was still at the same site that they were when he was wounded. He continued to supervise the building of the bridge and was later commended for leading his platoon in constructing the bridge under fire.

(Later, in the late 1940's, Berry started getting headaches and it was discovered that there were several fragments still in his head. The remaining fragments were removed at a military hospital at Fort Leonard Wood.)

*F Company floating a Bailey bridge section into position near Capua, Italy, March 1944.*

When Berry returned to duty in mid-February, his unit was still near San Angelo and the Allies were still trying to take Monte Casino in the same location that they had been two weeks earlier. He returned to the same fox hole and encountered the same daily fire from the Germans still holding out in the hills around the Monastery and on the surrounding mountain. The Germans endured daily bombing and assaults.

*A bridge built by F Company to carry a tank, near Cassino, Italy, February 1944.*

*A British truck stuck in the mud in the Liri River valley below Monte Cassino, January 1944. (12.)*

By early February the monks, about 1,500 refugees and local Italians that were living in the abbey were running out of food and water. Their stores were running low because the monks had not expected the many refugees that had arrived. The refugees included women and many children that were all scared and hungry. Shells and bombs landed around the abbey night and day and people were not allowed to leave by the Germans who were afraid that they would give away the positions of the Germans once they reached the Allied lines. (5.)

During the first two weeks of February, fighting continued to take place around the abbey. Troops from India and New Zealand managed to fight their way from the mountains on the Allied right to near the abbey. Fighting was ferocious and supplies were almost impossible to get to the men on the mountains. The Allies used donkeys to transport ammunition, rations and supplies to the men fighting on the mountains but the Germans killed hundreds of donkeys carrying supplies. Pressure on Mark Clark continued as his army was bogged down in front of the Gustav line at Monte Cassino. German artillery continued to stop men attempting to gain footholds and hand-to-hand fighting occurred in isolated mountain areas.

Finally, as evidence mounted that the Germans were occupying the abbey itself and were using the abbey to spot artillery and supply gun positions, General Clark authorized the aerial bombing of the abbey, much to the objection of the Pope and the church. Indian units had taken the heights above the abbey and officially requested the bombing of the abbey as prelude to a frontal assault.

*The Abbey of Monte Cassino after several days of bombing. The Allies bombed the abbey believing that the Germans occupied the abbey and were using it to spot artillery fire. However, there was not a single German killed by the bombing whereas over 200 civilians were killed. (14.)*

On February 15th, American B-17's flew a mission from the large military airport at Foggia, Italy and attacked the positions around the abbey and the abbey itself. After the first wave from Foggia dropped their bombs, a second wave of B-25's flew from Sardinia and dropped 1,000 pound bombs on the abbey. During the day of February 15th, 239 heavy and medium bombers dropped a total of 453 tons of bombs on the abbey, completely destroying it. As the bombers flew over and dropped their bombs, the men of the US Fifth Army and the British Eighth Army stood and cheered. Troops were frustrated from weeks of fighting with the false belief that the German defense was directed from the abbey itself. The bombing lasted for four solid hours. It is estimated that around 230 civilians, including many women and children, were killed by the bombs. There is no evidence that any Germans were killed or wounded from the attack, although the abbey was destroyed. Several monks were injured but none were killed. (5.)

The bombing occurred to help soften the German positions for the attack by the Indian troops. However, by the time the bombers had finished, the Indian troops did not attack. The abbey was bombed and destroyed for no reason.

*German Prisoners at the Battle of Cassino. (14.)*

Following the bombing, German paratroopers occupied the ruins of the abbey and used the ruins as protection for their positions. In March, the Indian troops were replaced by a division of Polish troops who continued the attack but were badly defeated by the dug-in Germans. The Germans held the ruins until May 18, 1944 when Polish troops finally took the abbey area (5.)

As the Allies were stalled at Monte Casino, Allied Command decided to perform an "end run" around Kesselring and to land behind the German lines at Anzio. The landing at Anzio forced ferocious fighting on both sides and eventually caused the Germans to retreat up the Italian boot. The 19th did not participate in the landing at Anzio but pushed forward up Route 6 with II Corps as the Germans retreated. After the break-out at Anzio, II Corps, including the 19th Engineers, advanced on Rome.

But, there were many more towns and cities to take and a large, well-equipped German army in the way. As the Allies pressed forward, and the men of 19th lead the way and were the first to enter many of the towns as they pushed north, clearing the way for the II Corps infantry units to press the attack. Fifth Army continued to slug it out with the retreating German Army as the Germans continually left mines and destroyed bridges to slow the Allied advance. But, the Allies pressed on to Rome.

*Colonel Killian, commander of 1st Battalion, 19th Engineer Regiment. Later, after the Battle of Kasserine Pass, Col Killian was named Commander of the 19th Engineer Regiment (Combat). After the war, he was G-1 for the Engineer Branch and helped Captain get his discharge papers.*

*Bombing of the town of Cassino. Below this photo in the referenced book, Lt Berry wrote, "I was about as close as this photographer when Cassino was bombed. I had a wonderful view – could feel the bombs burst." (12.)*

*Lt. Berry and Pvt. Bernie Smith of Reno, Nevada, with muddy boots, March 8, 1944, near Monte Cassino.*

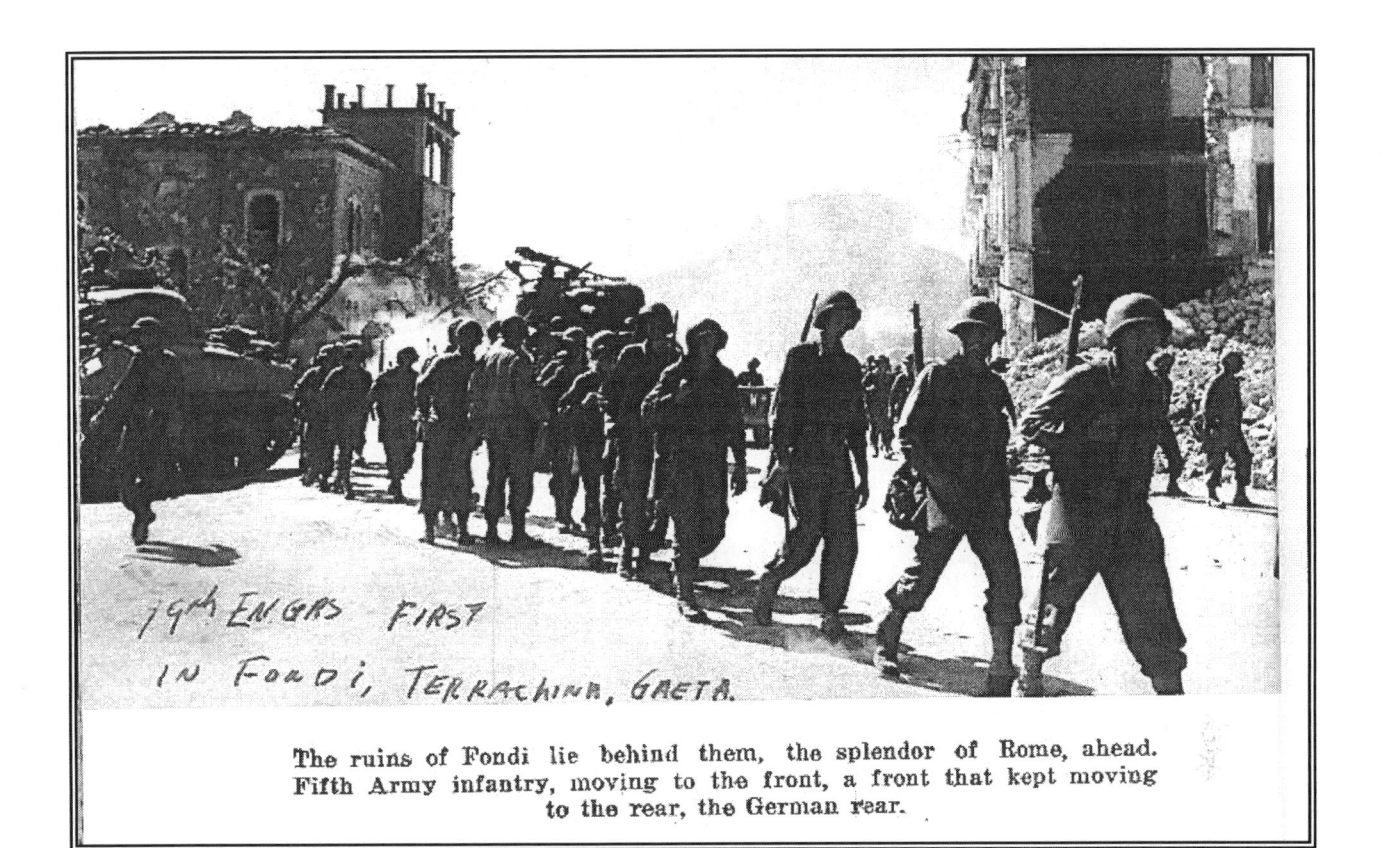

*[Handwritten on first photo:]* 19th ENGRS FIRST IN FONDI, TERRACINA, GAETA.

The ruins of Fondi lie behind them, the splendor of Rome, ahead. Fifth Army infantry, moving to the front, a front that kept moving to the rear, the German rear.

Tanks and infantry moving to jump-off positions for the break-through at the Fifth Army's Anzio beachhead. German tanks are wrecked hulks along the road.

*[Handwritten on second photo:]* TAPE DESIGNATES CLEAR LANES - done by 19th ENGRS UNDER FIRE.

*In the pamphlet, "Road To Rome" published by the US Military, Lt Berry wrote in the book about the white tape marking the cleared boundary of the road, "Tape designates clear lanes - done by 19th Engineers under fire."*

*Standing, Corporal Roe Betterton and MSgt George Bassett; sitting, Tech4 Robert Root and Pvt Ed Lewis, at Fondi, Italy, May 1944.*

*19th Engineers entering Rome with Italian civilians watching, June 6, 1944.*

General Clark is shown entering Rome with his Chief of Staff, Major General Alfred M. Gruenther (left rear) and the Rome Area Commander, Major General Harry H. Johnson. St. Peter's looms in the background.

*Later (after the previous photo was taken), General Mark Clark and his top generals entering Rome, June 6, 1944. (12.)*

*F Company floating a Bailey bridge section into position near Capua, Italy, March 1944.*

During March and April, Fifth Army regrouped and prepared for the Spring offensive toward Rome. General Clark assigned II Corps to cut the Minturno-Ausonia Road and to secure the foothills of the Petrella Mountains, and maintain pressure against the Germans in the direction of Formia. (12.) Fifth Army went on the final attack toward Rome on May 11, 1944. That night at 11:00, Allied artillery opened up from Cassino to the sea with a barrage of fire at the German lines. The men moved into position and prepared for the offensive that started just as the shelling stopped. All along the front, the Allies pushed.

The French Expeditionary Corps, now composed of the 2nd Moroccan Division, the 3rd Algerian Division, the 4th French Mountain Division and the 1st Motorized Division launched their offensive. American units attacked on the left and center. II Corps was in the coastal area and captured the towns of Scauri, Formia, Gaeta and Itri, which led toward Fondi and Rome.

*A new floating treadway bridge built on pontoons by F Company near Capua, Italy, March 1944.*

*Lt Berry receiving the Bronze Star from Maj General Keyes, Commander of II Corps, May 1944.*

The 19th Engineers was, as usual, in front of II Corps clearing the way for infantry and armored units. The 19th Engineers was the first unit to enter Fondi, Terracina and Gaeta. The Germans continued their withdrawal and prepared for the final defense of Rome. As II Corps advanced, they took Artena on May 28th and swung northwest toward the final stretch to Rome. At Valmontone, the German defenses were again broken and they could not continue their defense of Rome. German soldiers surrendered in droves leaving their equipment and vehicles abandoned along the road to Rome. The remainder of the German army retreated north past Rome leaving the first of three Axis power capitals to be taken without a fight.

As the engineers usually led the way, Lt Berry found himself to be one of the very first Allied soldiers to enter Rome on June 4, 1944, at the head of Fifth Army. The Germans continued to fight rear-guard actions but Rome was spared destruction and no combat occurred in the city. By the night of June 4th, the Allies had converged on all sectors of Rome and the first Axis capital city was in the hands of the Allies. As the Germans withdrew northerly, they were steadily hit by Allied aircraft. Meanwhile, Rome's citizens came out to enthusiastically meet the Allies entering the city.

Unfortunately, Lt Berry and the troops of the 19th could not stop to celebrate. They moved on to the north keeping pressure on the Germans and did not stop at all in Rome. Two days later, the Allies landed at Normandy.

During the drive to Rome, the US Fifth Army lost 107,144 men from January to June 4, 1944.

*Sgt Maxwell and Pfc Nix at the 19th Engineer water point near Mignano, Italy. Water points were set up for men to shower. Trips to the water point were quite a treat and offered a refreshing break from "spit baths" and shaving with cold water.*

*June 4, 1944, the 19th Engineers convoying through Rome as some of the very first Allied troops to enter Rome. Romans stand along the route and watch, some waving to the conquering Americans.*

*Cpt Berry enjoying some chow, near Rome, summer 1944.*

# On to the Po River

Fifth Army continued north from Rome to Florence. All along the way, the retreating Germans blew bridges and laid mines to slow the Allied advance. Those barriers gave the 19th plenty to do by clearing mines and rebuilding bridges – all in advance of the infantry and armored columns.

In the fall of 1944 Berry was promoted to Captain and assigned as 2d Battalion S-4 of the 19th Engineers which was headquartered near Florence, Italy. The battalion S-4 is responsible for supplies and logistics. He spent most of the later part of the war living near Florence. While there, he also served as special services officer which required him to go into Florence weekly. In March 1945, Berry was stationed near Bologna, Italy which was nearly the northern-most advance of the Allies before the end of the war.

*Cpt Berry, northern Italy, summer 1944.*

During one of his scrounging trips in the Fall of 1944, Captain Berry came across a beautiful new shotgun sitting behind a bar. Berry looked around and, naturally, assumed that the gun was abandoned so he took it and kept it with him for the next few weeks. Meanwhile, Lt Weed scrounged a nice desk and typewriter set that had beautiful inlaid wood. A few weeks later, Weed received orders to go home. He suddenly realized that there was no way he could take the desk set home with him and it was too late to have it shipped. He came to Berry and begged him to trade him for the shotgun. Finally, Berry gave in and Weed took the shotgun home with him with his gear. A few days later, lightning struck Berry's tent and destroyed the desk set.

While building bridges in Italy, the gaps that they would bridge would be many hundreds of feet above the valley floor. All of the troops were required to be tied-off with rope while they worked on the bridges. LTC. Kellogg, who was still the 2nd Battalion commander, never did tie himself off. He would walk those girders and never blink an eye.

During the Italian campaign, a lot of Italian people worked for the Allies doing things like cooking, kitchen police (KP) duty, truck mechanics, cutting hair, etc. The 19th would often set up the company mess halls in local churches. Churches were often intact and provided shelter for the weary men.

They moved forward every day as they fought through Italy toward the Alps.

*Lt. Berry, fourth from the left, about to receive the Bronze Star Medal for action in Tunisia in March 1943, from Maj General Keyes (partly hidden at the right), on the way to Rome, Italy, May 5, 1944.*

In May 1944, Lt Berry was ordered to attend an awards ceremony where he was awarded the Bronze Star and formally commended by Orders from Maj Gen Keyes, as follows:

"Jerome T. Berry, 0-4566507, 1st Lieutenant, Company F, 19th Engineer Regiment (Combat), for resourcefulness and outstanding leadership ability during the period **** to March 1943.

Lt Berry's platoon was given the job of reconstructing a railway overpass that had been completely demolished by retreating Germans one mile west of ****, Tunisia. He overcame the handicaps of serious lack of materials, lack of proper equipment, and small manpower by using his initiative which resulted in the bridge being completed ahead of schedule allowing vital army supplies to be moved forward to the front."

As the Allies advanced, the 19th Engineers advanced in front of the armored columns in order to clear the way. The engineers had one advantage though. As the day passed and the engineers went through a town in Italy they would look for a nice government building, which was often the town's opera house or the newly constructed headquarters for Mussolini's party. The engineers would erect signs around the perimeter of the building warning all that there were mines and booby traps within the building, even though there were actually none of the kind. As the infantry passed by, they steered clear of the building thinking that deadly booby traps waited within. Then, that evening, as their work was done, the engineers would go back to the building, remove the signs and have a nice, palatial place to sleep while the infantry was stuck in tents or in out buildings. Berry spent many nights comfortably cozy in a nice, new building built by the Fascist party in honor of Mussolini.

*Lt. Berry, receiving the Bronze Star Medal from Maj Gen Keyes, commander of II Corps, May, 1944.*

*Lt. Berry on R&R at Minturno, Italy, May 1944. Apparently, there were members of the Women's Army Corps nearby.*

Fall, 1944 Berry was promoted from 1st Lieutenant to Captain while the 19th was near Florence, Italy. Upon promotion, Berry was assigned as the regiment S-4, or Supply Officer. As supply officer, he was responsible for obtaining equipment, food, water, ammunition, uniforms and building supplies. Chief Warrant Officer (CWO) Francis served as Property Book Officer for Captain Berry. Berry had a hand-full of staff to help order and obtain supplies for the Regiment. Much of Berry's time during this period was spent finding supplies for the Regiment. Lumber was especially in short supply. The Army bought lumber and some other supplies from the local Italians. Sometimes, according to Berry, the Italians didn't want to sell – at least at the price offered by the Army. So, if they didn't want to sell, the US Army would just take it.

**Lt. Berry and Sgt Snow, relaxing a little, near Florence, summer 1944.**

**The caption on this postcard reads: "Military traffic streamed across the Volturno on temporary bridges like the one above at Capua. In the weeks just before the big drive was resumed in May."**

You could get movies but a movie projector was hard to come by. Luckily, engineer troops were issued special knives that all GI's wanted. Berry was able to trade 20 knives for a projector and the 19th was able to watch movies occasionally from then on.

168

*A Bailey bridge built by F Company in northern Italy, August 1944.*

As the Germans retreated north through Italy, they installed barriers as they went in order to delay the advance of the Allies. Barriers consisted mostly of destroying bridges and laying mine fields. The Army Engineers' primary mission is to remove barriers when the Army is on the offensive and to install barriers when the Army is retreating. So, most of the time in Italy was spent rebuilding bridges and clearing mine fields in support of the advancing Allies.

One of the strategies of war is to cover barriers that you install with fire. This strategy means that after destruction of a bridge or the installation of a mine field, the Germans covered the barrier with fire from infantry, artillery or mortars. Therefore, as the men of the 19th Engineers cleared mines, they were normally under fire from German forces. Needless to say, detecting and clearing mines is dangerous enough without having being fired upon at the same time.

*A postcard of the Arno River and the Ponte Vecchio at night in Florence, circa 1945.*

*A destroyed German tank, north of Florence, August, 1944.*

*Sgt George Bassett, Headquarters Company, 19th Engineers at regimental headquarters, July 1944.*

*Cpt Berry in Rome to see Joe Lewis fight Bob Berry, Spring 1945. Bob Berry, in this case was a soldier in Fifth Army that was a pretty good boxer who won the rights to take on Joe Lewis.*

Many destroyed bridges were remedied by building "shoe flies" which are detours or low water crossings next to the destroyed bridge. However, this was not possible to do in the mountains of Italy so most destroyed bridges in Italy were rebuilt by using Bailey Bridges. Bailey Bridges are bridges that are built from pre-fabricated metal assemblies. Metal pieces are hand-carried from a truck and assembled on an abutment. When the bridge is built, it is literally pushed by hand across the divide by the men. Bailey Bridges can be built to handle light foot or vehicular traffic or strong enough to hold heavy tanks and other armored vehicles. Destroyed bridges are also normally covered with fire. So, as the engineers build new bridges and try to put them in place, they can be under constant fire from various sources. When available and practical, smoke is used to cover the erection of the bridge by burning smoke pots up wind of the river crossing.

*Bernie Smith, a friend and classmate of Lt. Berry's at UNR, taken in Italy, 1944.*

*Men of the 19th Engineers enjoying a little Rest and Relaxation in Rome, December 15, 1944. Left to Right: Lt Meusch, Lt Buckner, Cpt Berry, Cpt Sesson, Cpt Phillips.*

*The US Army Band touring the front on the back of a 2.5-ton truck in southern Italy, 1944.*

*Captain Berry, In the mud in northern Italy, near Florence, December 1944.*

*Cpt Berry on Christmas Day, 1944, Northern Italy.*

*Cpt Berry in the snow of northern Italy, January 1945.*

*Captain Berry in the mud of northern Italy, Spring 1945. Somehow, he has acquired what look like "waders" although these were not issued by the Army. Perhaps his position of Battalion S-4 enabled him to obtain them.*

*These two photos were taken in December 1944 in central Italy near Florence. The person with Cpt Berry in the photo on the left is unknown. Notice the mud and the camp site.*

*Bridge constructed by F Company in the mountains of northern Italy, spring 1945.*

*Cpt Berry and friend, Lt. Buckner in northern Italy, February 1945.*

*Cpt Berry in the 19th Engineer bivouac site, Northern Italy, 1945.*

*Cpt. Berry in the mud of northern Italy, Spring 1945.*

*Bridge being built by F company in northern Italy. Notice the men in the lower right corner of the photo and the men sitting on top of the columns in the center of the gap.*

*Lt Mike Davoust. northern Italy. 1945.*

*Italians hung by Italians who were pro-Allied forces because they helped the Germans, near the Po River in Northern Italy, 1945.*

177

There were a number of opportunities to take some Rest and Relaxation (R & R) during the drive north past Rome. Many of the men of the 19th Engineers were given passes to visit Rome, including Berry and some other officers of the 19th in December 1944. They visited a few restaurants and were able to scrounge some wine which the Italians tried to hide.

*Cpt Berry, Spring, 1945, northern Italy.*

Of course, the bridge equipment had to be included in the supplies that disembarked from supply boats and then carried by truck from the harbor to the front lines. Long convoys of trucks were needed to carry bridge pieces to the front. As the Allies advanced, bridges that were well in the rear were often disassembled and then trucked to the front to bridge a new gap.

In March 1945, Berry received orders to come home to the United States. At that time, he was within a few miles of the Po River in Northern Italy near Bologna. Berry was replaced as Regimental S-4 by Vernon Loesing, who later was Berry's next door neighbor in Rolla, Missouri. Loesing was a career Army officer who retired in Rolla in the 1970's and became friends of Berry. It wasn't until several years after Loesing died that Berry learned that he was replaced by Loesing in 1945.

*Cpt Berry celebrating receipt of getting orders to come home in northern Italy, spring 1945. Notice II Corps patch on his left sleeve.*

*Catching a few at home, 1945.*

# Coming Home

Berry left Italy in late March and arrived at Boston, Massachusetts where he took a train to St. Louis and a bus to Rolla, arriving in early April 1945. He married Mary Frances Strawhun on April 14, 1945. His previous F company commander, Captain Pohlman was his best man. Biding his time in Rolla and enjoying his new wife and life, he waited for his expected discharge orders.

Sure enough, he soon received orders, but not to be discharged. He was assigned as the Utility Officer of the U.S. Army Hospital of Fort Sam Houston in San Antonio, Texas. So, he traveled to San Antonio, leaving his new wife behind in Rolla. When he reported, he again requested that he be discharged and he explained to the commanding officer that he was not a professional engineer and knew nothing about facilities engineering. The Commander understood and told Berry that he would try to get him re-assigned and/or discharged. In the meantime, he told Berry, go play some golf and check in every day to see if your orders have arrived.

## Reception To Honor Captain, Mrs. Berry

A RECEPTION at Mayflower hotel Saturday evening will honor Capt. and Mrs. Jerome Taylor Berry, newlyweds, and introduce Mrs. Berry to Akron friends of her husband.

The couple repeated nuptial vows at a ceremony solemnized recently in Rolla, Mo. Rev. E. M. Romine officiated at the wedding in the Rolla Methodist church.

Daughter of Mr. and Mrs. Walter L. Strawhum, the bride chose a two-piece suit of oyster-white wool trimmed with gold kidskin applique. She wore a white feather hat and carried a white prayer book bearing a fuchsia throated white orchid.

Miss Katherine and Miss Laura Berry of Akron, sisters of the bridegroom, attended the bride while Clarence Berry, brother of the bridegroom, served as best man. Ushers were Capt. Edgar F. Pohlmann and Lieut. Anthony Meile, who served with Captain Berry in a combat engineer battalion overseas for 30 months.

An open house will be held Sunday at the home of the bridegroom's parents, Mr. and Mrs. C. W. Berry, 1776 Marks av., honoring the couple.

Following their Akron visit, Captain Berry will rejoin the 19th engineers in Italy. His bride will resume her position in the registrar's office at the School of Mines, Rolla.

**CAPTAIN AND MRS. BERRY**

*The wedding party on April 14, 1945 in Rolla, Missosuri. From left to right: Lt. Anthony Melle, Cpt Ed Pohlmann, Mary Frances Strawhun Berry, Cpt Jerry Berry, Katherine Berry (Jerry's sister) and Lauretta Berry (Jerry's other sister).*

So, Berry took off for the links, with a wife back home in Rolla and with visions of a discharge on the immediate horizon. He ordered a 2d Lieutenant to check the posting of orders every day and to report to him if any orders were posted for him. After several days of playing golf, Berry looked up one day while on the golf course, and saw the 2d Lieutenant coming toward him in a jeep. He told Berry that he, indeed, had orders posted. Berry sped to see his discharge date but, as the Army tends to do, he was again surprised.

Berry was assigned as the new camp commander of a prisoner of war camp at Camp Claiborne, near Alexandria, Louisiana! So, in early May 1945, Berry took a train from San Antonio to Alexandria, Louisiana to take command of the prisoner of war camp. Soon after he arrived, the war in Europe ended with the unconditional surrender of Germany. Soon after VE day, he sent for his new wife and he and Mary Frances set up house at Camp Claiborne.

COL Killian, who had been commander of the 19th Engineer Regiment, was now assigned as the G-1 of the Engineer Branch at the Pentagon. Captain Berry contacted COL Killian who said that he would help get Berry's orders changed. Meanwhile, Mary Fran went to Camp Claiborne and enjoyed it there. It was spring but hot in southern Louisiana and she was able to spend lots of time by the pool where she met other officers' wives. "They mostly played Bridge and ate shrimp", according to Dad.

The Berry's set up house for a few weeks while Captain Berry tried to get out of the Army. He called Colonel Killian again and retold him that he really wanted out of the Army and if he couldn't get a discharge, he at least wanted to be assigned to Fort Leonard Wood. Finally, near the end of May 1945, Berry got orders to report to Fort Leonard Wood.

*Cpt and Mrs. Berry cutting the cake with Katherine Berry watching, April 14, 1945.*

For the first few days, he was assigned as the commander of an African-American engineer battalion at Fort Leonard Wood. Prior to 1951, African-Americans were in separate units, usually commanded by white officers.

He was sure that he would be discharged from the Army any day. However, the war in the Pacific was still raging and there were thoughts of millions of Americans storming the shores of Japan under heavy fire. Then, he was assigned as the Fort Wood Maintenance Officer for a few days. He was sent a new 2d Lieutenant to be his assistant and when he arrived he came to report to Berry and reported as "Ralph Truman", nephew of (then) President Truman. Berry continued to request to be discharged so that he could attend college in Rolla at what was then called the Missouri School of Mines (MSM).

Jerry spent the Fall of 1945 in the Army at Ft. Leonard Wood while Mary Fran continued working at MSM. They spent time at the Fort taking advantage of the Officer's Club and other facilities there.

*Cpt Jerry Berry met his new wife at the Alexandria, Louisiana train station for their brief stay at Camp Claiborne.*

Jerry and Mary Fran decided to try to live in or near Rolla. Jerry worked at Fort Wood hoping each day that he would be discharged. He wanted desperately to go to college and the Missouri School of Mines, a great engineering school, was located in Rolla. (The school is now known as the University of Missouri – Rolla (UMR)). World War II finally ended on August 10, 1945 with the surrender of Japan and Jerry was discharged from active duty in December 1945 in time to enroll as a student at (now) UMR for the Spring semester.

He signed up for the MSM varsity football team and went to school from January 1946 through May 1949. In 1948, he took a job as a technician at the United State Geological Survey (USGS) which had its offices in the Civil Engineering Building (Harris Hall) at MSM. Berry would attend classes in the same building and then work afternoons, evenings and nights in the same building on a different floor. He finally graduated in May 1949 one day before I was born.

# Epilogue

While Jerry went to college and Mary Fran continued to work at UMR, they lived in a small apartment next to Walter's tire shop at the corner of 9th (301 West 9th Street) and Rolla Streets.

Jerry took a part-time job with the United States Geological Survey, in Rolla, before he graduated and usually worked nights while Mary Fran worked days. Finally, in May 1949, Jerry graduated with a bachelor of science in Civil Engineering. He immediately accepted an offer as a civil engineer with the USGS in Rolla from where he retired in 1978.

Jerry stayed in the Army Reserves for over twenty years. He eventually made the rank of Major. He retired from the Army Reserve in 1969.

*August 1947, the Berry's took a trip to South Dakota, the Rockies, Yellowstone Park, Salt Lake City, the Badlands, and other points "out west".*

*Mary Fran fishing in a wet boat with heels and a cute sun dress in 1947.*

My mother died on July 5, 1997 from complications of lung cancer and several severe strokes. I was with her when she died.

My father died on July 8, 2005, just as I finished this book. He got to read the final draft but did not see the finished book. Although we wrote it together, he did all of the work. He spent four years fighting the greatest war in the history of mankind. He joins my mother, and Clarence Fulton, and Alphonso Rocco and Charlie Ellis and Wilson Withers and Ray Palmquist and his many other buddies who died in World War II.

*Jerry Berry as a student at MSM and a member of the varsity football team, fall 1947.*

*Officers and men of dad's US Army Reserve unit enjoying a meal. Major Berry is at "12 O'Clock" and COL Le Compte Joslin, commander of the unit, is second from the left of Berry. The other members are unknown.*

*Men of F company, 19th Engineers at a reunion in San Francisco, 1986. Left to Right: Jerry and Mary Fran Berry; Mewshaws; Killians; Williamsons; and, McHughs.*

*Major Berry during a reserve weekend, around 1964.*

**Ed Pohlmann** Dad's company commander during WWII, served as Berry's best man. He moved to College Park, Maryland after the war and died there in the 1980's.

**Justin Merriman** Merriman was in 3rd Platoon of F Company and ended up as a good friend of Berry. He has remained active with the 19th Engineer reunions and lives today (as of 2005) in Arizona.

**Bob Weed** He served as a platoon leader with Dad in F Company and later transferred to E Company. He was transferred to a garrison post in the United States during the Italian campaign and lives today (as of 2005) in Arizona. He wrote a book of his memoirs in World War II with the 19th Engineers called "In time of War".

**Emil Buckner** and his wife Claudia live as of 2005, in Great Neck, New York.

**Fred Theiss**, F. Company Platoon Sergeant, lived in Tuscon, Arizona with his wife, Evelyn, as of 2005.

**Lyle and Wilma Pittenger** lived in Jackson, Ohio. Lyle died on January 10, 1995

**Jacob Kuntz** Served in F Company, 3rd Platoon. He lived in Jamestown, North Dakota as of 2005.

**Robert Taylor Berry:** Mary Fran and Jerry lived together at 301 West 9th Street in Rolla while Jerry finished school and Mary Fran worked at MSM. I was born on May 22, 1949, just a few days after Jerry graduated from MSM with a civil engineering degree. He continued to work at the USGS as a civil engineer instead of a technician. We moved to our first house at 1019 Lynwood Drive in 1951, I think, when I was two. Lynwood Drive was part of the Ridgeview Subdivision and the house exists today much as it was in the 1950's.

I graduated in 1967 from Rolla High School. Like both my mother and father, in 1967, I enrolled at MSM/UMR as a freshman and like my father, graduated with a bachelors in civil engineering in 1972. Also like my dad, I took Reserve Officer's Training Corps training while at UMR and when I graduated, I accepted a Regular Army commission as a 2d Lieutenant.

*Dad and I, Rolla, Missouri, around 1953.*

*2Lt Berry being sworn in with a Regular Army commission at Fort Riley, Kansas, 1st Infantry Division, August, 1972.*

Like my grandfather, my first assignment was with the 1st Infantry Division in Ft. Riley, Kansas; 1st Engineer Battalion, 1st Infantry Division – "First of the First". And, like my father, I soon got orders to attend the Engineer Officer Basic Course in Ft. Belvoir, Virginia. Dad was in class #3 – I was in class #94.

After graduating from EOBC, like my father and my grandfather I served in Europe as part of the "Army of Occupation". Unlike my father and grandfather, however, I was in charge of a nuclear weapons unit. Also unlike my father and grandfather, no one shot at me. I served in what we used to call the "Cold War" whereas they served in "hot" ones.

Like my father and grandfather, I took advantage of the GI Bill and let the military pay for further education, allowing me to graduate with master's degrees and a doctor of engineering from the University of Kansas.

Like my father, I stayed in the Army Reserve, from 1976 through 1993, assigned to the 416th Engineer Command. Within that command, I served as a platoon leader of the 471st Engineer Company, an asphalt production and road building company and as a team member of engineer survey teams in Kansas City and St. Louis. I retired as a Lieutenant Colonel in 1993.

On February 27,1981, I married June Humber Schlanker. We had twin daughters, Katherine Trabue and

*Christmas 1949 at the house on Rolla Street. Mom, Dad and me.*

Carolyn Marie, born on June 3, 1983. Every time I went out of town on reserve duty, the twins got sick and June had to deal with them alone. I could never convince either daughter to polish my boots.

Carrie and Katie are both happy and living free and dealing with a world that remains troubled and violent. But more countries become free and governing as democracies every year. My father and grandfather would be proud that they had a role in that.

**Colleen Marie Berry** was born of Jerry and Mary Fran Berry on April 29, 1954 in Rolla, Missouri. She was named after her grandmother, Ruth Marie, who had died three years earlier. Like her mother, she went to grade school and secondary school in Rolla, graduating from Rolla High School in 1972. Also like her mother, she went to college at the University of Missouri at Columbia, graduating in 1976.

Also like her mother, she met her eventual husband, Kim, while a student at Mizzou. Later she graduated with a masters degree in speech pathology from what is now Truman State University in Kirksville, Missouri. In May 1980, she married Kim Scott Anderson in the same church that her mother was married in: the United Methodist Church in Rolla.

Colleen and Kim's daughter, Kelly Marie Anderson, also named after her mother and her grandmother, was born on July 31, 1984 in St. Louis, Missouri. She is currently living in St. Louis with her husband and daughter.

*Colleen and I in our front yard in Rolla, on the way to Sunday School, 1958.*

*The British cemetery of men who died in southern Italy during World War II, lies in the shadows of Monte Cassino, where many of them died, and which again shoulders the Abbey of Monte Cassino. This photo taken in May 2005.*

**The Abbey of Monte Cassino** was rebuilt in the 1940's and 1950's and most of the Abbey's artifacts, art and valuables have been returned. Construction of the Abbey was partly paid for by American donations. Volumes of research have concluded that the Germans were not occupying the Abbey during or before the Battle of Monte Cassino and the total destruction of the Abbey was unwarranted. The Abbey exists today overlooking the Liri and Rapido valleys just as it did in 529 AD when it was originally founded. It also overlooks an Allied cemetery in San Angelo which contains the remains of thousands of British soldiers. American dead from the battles of southern Italy are buried nearby at Anzio.

Nearby flows the Rapido and Liri Rivers, crossed daily by thousands of travelers who can barely imagine the fighting and carnage that took place on their banks. Also nearby, the modern Italian Autostrada provides six lanes of traffic to flow unimpeded to the heart of Rome, built along the Liri Valley and on the site of the ancient Appian Way, the route the 19th Engineers took to first occupy Rome in 1944.

*A bridge over the Rapido River near San Angelo, Italy, taken in May 2005. Jerry Berry was wounded very close to here in February 1944 while trying to supervise the construction of a different bridge across the Rapido.*

**The Rapido River near San Angelo, Italy.** Today, the Rapido flows through Italian cities of Caserta, Cassino and San Angelo, among many others, hardly noticed by thousands of travelers crossing the hundreds of bridges over it.

**The 19th Engineer Regiment** The 19th Engineer Regiment (Combat) has its roots as the 39th Engineers which was constituted in preparation for the US entering World War I on 15 August 1917. It was organized at Camp Upton, New York on February 18, 1918. The unit was converted and reorganized as the 39th Regiment, Transportation Corps on September 7, 1918 and then broken up and reorganized as the 26th Company, Transportation Corps at Camp Jackson, on July 11, 1919. On October 1, 1933, the unit was reconstituted in the regular army of the United States as the 39th Engineers.

The unit was activated at Fort Ord, California on June 1, 1940, shortly before 2Lt. Berry joined it. It was reorganized and redesignated as the 19th Engineers on July 1, 1940 and redesignated the 19th Engineer Regiment (Combat) on August 1, 1942 while the unit was in Camp Kilmer.

After World War II, the regiment was broken up on March 1, 1945 (when Berry was ordered home) into various engineer units. 1st Battalion of the 19th became the 401st Engineer Battalion (Combat) and 2d Battalion became the 402nd Engineer Battalion (Combat). The 401st was deactivated on December 6, 1945 at Camp Polk, Louisiana and was re-designated at the 52d Engineer Battalion on January 30, 1947. It was reactivated on November 27, 1951 at Fort Leonard Wood, Missouri and again deactivated in 1956.

On February 21, 1968, the unit was again activated at Fort Carson, Colorado.

The unit received campaign ribbons for World War I, World War II, Vietnam and during Desert Storm.

*The famous Ponte Vecchio, built in the 1500's stands today as a tourist and shopping Mecca in the heart of Florence. My wife and daughter, June and Carrie, enjoy the scene.*

**Florence, Italy** Today, as it was before the war, Florence is one of the great cities on earth and millions of visitors yearly enjoy its art, antiquities, architecture and history. Many visitors will cross the Ponte Vecchio which, unlike all of the other bridges across the Arno, was sparred destruction by the Germans. Just to the south of the Ponte Vecchio stands the Pitti Palace, used by Fifth Army as its headquarters during the campaign in northern Italy. Captain Berry attended many meetings in the Palace which stands today as home to art and history for all to see.

*Bob Berry outside of the Pitti Palace in Florence, May 2005.*

***The Robert Berry family and the Colleen Anderson family live free today, along with millions of other people, thanks to the sacrifices made by the men and women who served with the Allied forces during World War II. And now, they get to read and see a few pictures of their story.***

# References

(1.) Weed, Robert C., "In Time of War", Banner Printing, 1990.

(2.) Atkinson, Rick, "An Army at Dawn", Henry Holt and Company, 2002.

(3.) Blumenson, Martin, "Kasserine Pass", Houghton Mifflin C., 1967.

(4.) Goralski, Robert, "World War II Almanac", Bonanza Books, 1981.

(5.) Hapgood, David, and Richardson, David, "Monte Cassino", Congdon & Weed, 1984.

(6.) Badsey, Stephen and the Royal Military Academy Sandhurst, "Atlas of World War II Battle Plans", Barnes & Noble, New York, 2000.

(7.) Majdalany, Fred, "The Battle of Cassino", Ballantine Books, 1957.

(8.) "The Picture History of World War II, 1939-1945", Grosset & Dunlap, 1946.

(9.) Bond, Harold L., "Return to Cassino, A Memoir of the Fight for Rome", Doubleday & Company, New York, 1964.

(10.) Whiting, Charles, "Kasserine, The Battlefield Slaughter of American Troops by Rommel's Africa Korps", Dorsett Press, New York, 1984.

(11.) Breuer, William B., "Drop Zone Sicily, Allied Airborne Strike, July 1943", Presidio Press, Navato, California, 1983.

(12.) "Road to Rome", written by Headquarters, US Fifth Army, 1944.

(13.) Moorehead, Alan, "The March to Tunis, the North African War, 1940-1943", Harper & Row, New York, 1967.

(14.) "Life – World War 2, History's Greatest Conflict in Pictures", edited by Stolley, Richard B., A Bulfinch Press Book.

(15.) Ellis, John, "Cassino, The Hollow Victory", Sphere Books, Limited, London and Sydney, 1984.

# Index

1st Air Landing Brigade British......................103
1st Armored Division.........42, 45, 46, 61, 76, 89
1st Infantry Division ....2, 42, 50, 61, 69, 86, 104, 108, 189
1st Motorized Division ...............................161
1st Ranger Division ........................................46
2nd Armor Division...........................................41
2nd Moroccan Division ..................................161
3rd Algerian Division.......................................161
3rd Infantry Division...............................41, 104
4th French Mountain Division .......................161
5th Panzer Division, German ............................61
9th Infantry Division................................41, 86
10th Panzer Division, German ........56, 57, 69, 71
14th Panzer Corps, German ............122, 125, 134
16th Infantry Division..............................46, 51
18th Army ..............................................72, 91, 104
18th Infantry Division...............................46, 50, 58
19th Engineer
    Regiment..i, ii, v, 1, 24, 26, 27, 42, 47, 57, 64, 68, 69, 71, 104, 108, 122, 129, 134, 166, 188
19th Engineer Regiment....................................**192**
19th Engineers
    Regiment.....32, 42, 50, 60, 61, 69, 70, 71, 74, 76, 84, 91, 105, 108, 114, 126, 129, 135, 143, 145, 146, 148, 154, 162, 169, 178, 188
21st Panzer Division, German ..61, 62, 69, 72, 86
27th Basic Training Battalion ...........................18
36th Infantry Division................................145, 146
45th Infantry Division.....................104, 108, 134
82d Airborne Division ...........................103, 107
102d Airborne Division ...................................108
601st CAM Engineer Battalion...........................24
Africa Korps German........14, 40, 54, 69, 71, 195
Alexander, British General .69, 72, 91, 103, 122, 125
Allen,
    Gen Terry Allen 42, 45, 46, 48, 49, 50, 61, 69, 104
Allfrey, British General .......................58, 61, 91

Anderson
    British General................................64, 68, 70, 76
    Kelly Marie...................................................190
    Kim................................................................190
Antrim, Scotland ...............................30, 31, 32
Anzio, Italy ..............................................144, 154
Arnim, German General....................................94
Arzew
    Algeria ..45, 46, 48, 49, 51, 52, 54, 55, 59, 60, 94
Berry ...6, 7, 8, 16, 18, 22, 27, 32, 33, 34, 35, 48, 51, 52, 53, 54, 55, 60, 61, 69, 71, 85, 94, 110, 111, 114, 122, 146, 147, 148, 150, 162, 165, 166, 168, 179, 181, 182, 183
    Carolyn Marie...............................................190
    Clarence and Fannie .......................................7
    Clarence Washington......................................6
    Colleen Marie ..............................................190
    Jerome Taylor..i, 6, 7, 8, 9, 10, 13, 17, 18, 21, 22, 24, 26, 27, 28, 29, 31, 32, 33, 34, 35, 36, 47, 48, 49, 51, 54, 59, 60, 61, 64, 85, 86, 105, 108, 111, 126, 134, 166, 168, 178, 188
    Katherine Trabue .........................................189
    Mary Frances ..21, 22, 34, 183, 184, 185, 188, 190
    Walter Scott .....................................................6
Big Red One...............................................86, 89, 108
Bizerte
    Algeria, Port of .38, 53, 54, 56, 61, 84, 89, 91, 94, 105
Bob Weed.................................................26, 188
Bradley, Gen Omar 38, 76, 87, 91, 104, 108, 122
British Eighth Army..14, 84, 103, 105, 108, 122, 125, 126, 138, 153
British V Corps ..................................................64
Buckner, Lt Emile.....................27, 61, 94, 188
Camp Claiborne ......................................182, 183
Camp Kilmer............................................26, 27
Cassino
    Monte....3, 126, 138, 141, 143, 147, 152, 161, 195

196

Churchill, Sir Winston ............. 13, 15, 16, 40, 51
Clarence Lou Berry ............................................... 7
Clarence Fulton ..................................................... ii
Clark
    Gen Mark ...... 38, 42, 122, 125, 134, 142, 143, 146, 152, 161
Coldstream Guards, British ............................... 58
Conrath, German General .............................. 103
Darlan, Admiral ..................................... 51, 52, 54, 58
Davoust, Lt Mike ................................................ 61
Dunkirk, Battle of ................................. 12, 30, 40
Eisenhower ......................................................... 104
    Gen Dwight 38, 41, 42, 52, 57, 58, 59, 61, 73, 76, 77, 84, 91, 94, 103, 122
El Guettar, Battle of ........................ 38, 86, 87, 89
Ellis
    Charles or Charlie ..... ii, 26, 27, 32, 34, 35, 85, 86, 111, 195
Faid Pass, Battle of ............ 38, 56, 61, 64, 66, 75
Fannie Taylor, Berry ............................................ 6
Fifth Army ...... 52, 114, 122, 125, 129, 134, 136, 142, 145, 153, 161, 162, 165, 195
Fondouk Pass, Tunisia, Battle of ..................... 90
Fort Belvoir ................................................. 21, 22
Fort Belvoir. ........................................................ 21
Fort Douglas, Utah ....................................... 10, 16
Fort Ord .................................................... 24, **192**
Francis, Chief Warrant Officer ..................... 168
Fredendall
    Maj Gen Lloyd . 27, 41, 45, 61, 62, 63, 64, 66, 67, 68, 69, 72, 76
French Foreign Legion ................................ 50, 53
Fulton, Private Clarence O ............................... 71
Gafsa, Tunisia, Battle of ................. 66, 84, 86, 87
Gela, Sicily ....................................... 103, 107, 108
Goering ............................................................. 142
Great Depression ................................................. 7
Gustav, Line ... 125, 134, 138, 141, 143, 145, 152
Guzzoni, Italian General Alfredo ... 102, 105, 107
Hanrahan, John F. ....................................... ii, 111
Hawkins, Captain Murf ..................................... 61
Hermann Goering Division ............ 103, 134, 141
Hewlett, Private .................................................. 33
Hill 609, Battle of ........................................ 38, 91
Hitler, Adolph ..................... 12, 51, 102, 121, 141

II Corps 27, 57, 61, 63, 64, 66, 67, 68, 72, 74, 75, 76, 77, 84, 85, 86, 87, 89, 90, 91, 104, 107, 110, 122, 125, 126, 134, 145, 154, 161, 162
Ike, General Dwight D. Eisenhower .......... 57, 59
Kasserine Pass ... 2, 38, 63, 64, 66, 67, 68, 69, 71, 72, 74, 195
Kellogg, LTC ........................ 34, 35, 52, 60, 165
Kesselring
    Field Marshall Herman ...... 102, 121, 122, 125, 138, 142, 144, 154
Kewpie's ............................................................... 8
Keyes, Gen Geoffrey .............................. 122, 166
Killian ..................................................... **182, 183**
Longstop Hill, Tunisia, Battle of ............... 58, 61
Mankoweicz, Lt ................................................. 61
Marion Motley ..................................................... 9
Mary Frances Strawhun ......................... 181, 182
nMerriman, Sgt Justin ..................................... 188
Minturno, Italy ......................................... 144, 161
Mockler-Ferryman, Gen Eric ........................... 76
Monte
    Cassino, Battle of .. 3, 138, 141, 143, 147, 150, 152, 154, 195
Monte Cassino .............................................. **191**
Montgomery
    Gen Bernard L. . 14, 38, 40, 42, 59, 84, 86, 91, 103, 110, 122, 125
Moore, Col ATW ........................... ii, 42, 60, 68, 71
Mussolini ................... 12, 51, 104, 105, 121, 166
O'Neil's Department Store ................................ 8
Oberon, Merle ................................................... 32
Operation Husky ............................................. 103
Operation Reservist ........................................... 45
Operation Torch ................................. 15, 40, 54
Operation Trojan Horse ................................ 102
Oran
    Algeria .. 38, 41, 42, 45, 50, 51, 52, 53, 54, 55, 60, 105
Patton
    General George. 38, 41, 52, 76, 77, 84, 85, 86, 87, 89, 91, 103, 105, 108, 110, 122
Pearl Harbor ............................... 13, 18, 22, 25
Petain, Marshall Philippe ................................. 12
Pohlman, Captain Edgar .......... 26, 27, 34, 61, 85
Pohlmann, Captain Edgar ...................... 111, 188
Queen Elizabeth .................................. 27, 29, 30

Rapido
- River, Italy, Battle of 138, 141, 142, 143, 144, 145, 146, 147

Read-Benzol Company ........................................ 7
Red Devil Brigade............................................ 103
Relizane, Algeria............................. 55, 56, 60, 61
Rolla
- Missouri .. 18, 21, 22, 179, 181, 182, 183, 185, 188, 190

Rommel ..... 54, 61, 66, 68, 69, 70, 71, 72, 74, 76, 77, 121
- General Erwin................................ 13, 15, 195
- Marshall Erwin .............. 38, 40, 42, 49, 52, 59

Roosevelt
- Franklin D................................. 15, 16, 40, 143
- Gen Theodore .......... 14, 15, 40, 42, 45, 50, 51

San Angelo, Italy, Battle of.... 145, 146, 147, 150
San Pietro, Italy, Battle of.............................. 134
Sant' Angelo, Italy, Battle of ........................ 143
Sbeitla, Tunisia, Battle of......... 64, 66, 67, 68, 74
Schlanker, June Humber ................................ 189
Sckorupski, John .............................................. 71
Senger
- German General Frido von ....... 102, 121, 125, 134, 138, 142, 144

Seventh Army American.......... 103, 105, 110, 122
Shirley. Lt Jack ................................................ 61
Sidi Bel Abbes, Algeria ..................... 53, 54, 55
Sidi bou Zid, Tunisia, Battle of............ 66, 67, 68
Spaatz, Lt Gen Carl.......................................... 87
St. Cloud, Algeria, Battle of...................... 50, 51
Stark, Col Alexander............................. 69, 71, 76
Superga, Division, Italian ............................... 57
Taylor
- Boyce........................................................... 7
- Charlie ........................................................ 7
- Fannie Cornelia .......................................... 6

Tedder, British Air Marshall............................ 87
Truscott, Gen Lucien ............................... 38, 104
USS Washington............................................... 35
Vichy
- Vichy French .... 12, 13, 38, 41, 42, 45, 47, 48, 49, 50, 51, 53, 54

Volturno, River, Italy.................................... 129
Ward, Gen Orlando................... ii, 45, 67, 76, 89
Weed, Bob 1, 26, 27, 35, 55, 61, 94, 95, 165, 195
Withers, Wilson V. .............................. ii, 27, 111
Wood
- Fort Leonard ... 1, 13, 16, 17, 18, 21, 150, 181, 183, 184

Made in the USA
Columbia, SC
20 April 2018